Historical Studies in Education

Series Editors
William J. Reese
Department of Educational Policy Studies
University of Wisconsin-Madison
Madison, Wisconsin, USA

John L. Rury
University of Kansas
Lawrence, Kansas, USA

This series features new scholarship on the historical development of education, defined broadly, in the United States and elsewhere. Interdisciplinary in orientation and comprehensive in scope, it spans methodological boundaries and interpretive traditions. Imaginative and thoughtful history can contribute to the global conversation about educational change. Inspired history lends itself to continued hope for reform, and to realizing the potential for progress in all educational experiences.

More information about this series at
http://www.springer.com/series/14870

Peter Otiato Ojiambo

Kenyan Youth Education in Colonial and Post-Colonial Times

Joseph Kamiru Gikubu's Impact

Peter Otiato Ojiambo
Lawrence, Kansas
USA

Historical Studies in Education
ISBN 978-3-319-86753-3   ISBN 978-3-319-59990-8   (eBook)
DOI 10.1007/978-3-319-59990-8

© The Editor(s) (if applicable) and The Author(s) 2017
Softcover reprint of the hardcover 1st edition 2017
This work is subject to copyright. All rights are solely and exclusively licensed by the Publisher, whether the whole or part of the material is concerned, specifically the rights of translation, reprinting, reuse of illustrations, recitation, broadcasting, reproduction on microfilms or in any other physical way, and transmission or information storage and retrieval, electronic adaptation, computer software, or by similar or dissimilar methodology now known or hereafter developed.
The use of general descriptive names, registered names, trademarks, service marks, etc. in this publication does not imply, even in the absence of a specific statement, that such names are exempt from the relevant protective laws and regulations and therefore free for general use.
The publisher, the authors and the editors are safe to assume that the advice and information in this book are believed to be true and accurate at the date of publication. Neither the publisher nor the authors or the editors give a warranty, express or implied, with respect to the material contained herein or for any errors or omissions that may have been made. The publisher remains neutral with regard to jurisdictional claims in published maps and institutional affiliations.

Cover illustration: © epicurean/E+/getty images

Printed on acid-free paper

This Palgrave Macmillan imprint is published by Springer Nature
The registered company is Springer International Publishing AG
The registered company address is: Gewerbestrasse 11, 6330 Cham, Switzerland

*To the three Founders of Starehe Boys Centre and School—Geoffrey Griffin,
Geoffrey Geturo, and Joseph Gikubu—for giving the Kenyans youth
education. The Kenyan nation is so grateful for your contribution.
AND
For Njenga, Karanja, Ada, Bella and other grand-children in the hope that
your children will read this book and get to know their great-grandfather and
the role he played
in the growth of Kenyan youth education.*

SERIES FOREWORD

The history of education on the African continent has received far too little consideration in recent years. Despite a rising interest in colonialism as a historical problem, and the increasing attention devoted to the "global south" and subaltern studies, the development of schools and other educational institutions in this critically important part of the world remains under studied. Peter Otiato Ojiambo offers an example of the sort of study that can begin to address this problem, carefully focusing on the careers of important educational leaders in Kenya and their impact on that nation's youth and educational institutions.

Joseph Kamiru Gikubu was a visionary leader and institution builder at a time when Kenya was making the transition from British colony to independent, postcolonial nation and society. Along with his colleagues Geoffrey William Griffin and Geoffrey Gatama Geturo, he was moved by the problems posed by youth in the militant Mau Movement during the latter stages of the colonial period, recognizing the need for stable and nurturing educational institutions to address their needs. This led to a career in serving apparently wayward juveniles in a variety of settings and circumstances. The culmination of this work was the founding of the Starehe Boys Centre and School, an institution that became well known and continues to operate in Nairobi today.

In addition to discussing Gikubu's work and influence, Professor Ojiambo paints a vivid picture of the conditions facing Kenyan youth and the nation's schools during a critical stage of African history. In this respect, this work of educational biography represents a telling contribution to the history of African education. It also demonstrates the vital role that resolute and praiseworthy leaders can play in creating pathways for subsequent generations to realize their potential and contribute to the continent's advancement. The institutions that emerge from such efforts can bolster the forces of positive, equitable social change that doubtless represents the best hope for its future.

Madison, USA William J. Reese
Lawrence, USA John L. Rury

Preface

The development and growth of Kenyan youth education has been shaped by various educational actors, some known and others unknown. To effectively comprehend this subject, it is imperative to examine the contributions of the two primary actors. This book examines the assertion that a biography can focus on individuals who might be in one sense of relatively little importance but despite this can be cited as an archetype or as a useful way into issues and developments that have wider historical importance. Joseph Kamiru Gikubu, the main subject of this book, is a man of relatively humble background who distinguished himself in the field of Kenyan youth education, yet limited biographical research work exists on his contributions to Kenyan education. This is an omission that this book sets out to correct, examining as it does his role in the growth of Kenyan youth education in both the colonial and postcolonial periods. But why do we need a biographical appraisal of Joseph Gikubu at all?

This book notes that Gikubu is an important figure in the growth of Kenyan youth education. It asserts that for 55 years he played an active role not only in building and improving Kenyan youth education but also in demonstrating the role that educational institutions can play in imparting nation-building skills and responsible citizenship in youth. Gikubu's educational contributions were wide ranging, including practical and theoretical aspects of education as well as the effective administration of learning institutions. Further, his contributions looked at the ways in which holistic, engaged, critical, and cohesive learning communities can be created. Specifically, the book examines Gikubu's involvement in Kenyan youth education through his work in the juvenile rehabilitation programs at Manyani detention camp, Wamumu rehabilitation camp, Starehe youth club, Kariokor youth club, Othaya Approved School, and Starehe Boys Centre and School, and his insights into the purpose of education, educational leadership, and strategies that can be utilized to create effective teaching and learning institutions. In addition, through examining Gikubu's contributions to Kenyan youth education, the book seeks to interrogate Kenya's educational history and policy in the colonial and postcolonial periods, its transformation, progress, challenges, and prospects.

This is an attempt to fill the gap in African-centered educational biographies that show how educators shaped Africa's social, political, and economic spheres in both the colonial and postcolonial periods. It provides a synopsis of the growing research interest in this area and indicates the challenges that are entailed. It analyzes the significance of those educators whose contributions to the growth of African education is immense yet poorly documented. This is the book's unique niche in terms of its contribution to African educational biographical studies. It is hoped that it will go some way towards addressing the research and intellectual needs of this steadily evolving field, whether in Kenya, in Africa, or globally. Educators, scholars, students, administrators, policymakers, and community leaders engaged in the field of education will find *Kenyan Youth Education in Colonial and Post-Colonial Times: Joseph Gikubu's Impact* a significant resource for their work.

Lawrence, KS Peter Otiato Ojiambo
USA

ACKNOWLEDGMENTS

I would like to thank all those who helped me write this book. First, I would like to thank the Gikubu family both for their interest, excitement, and generous spirit, and for affirming the project's importance. Special thanks go to Diane Ciekawy, who challenged me soon after my doctoral studies to undertake the project and underscored its significance in the field of African-centered educational biographies. I am also grateful to the Director of Starehe Boys Centre and School, Matthew Kithyaka, and the entire faculty for receiving me at the school for several years and providing me with the required materials for this biography. Further, I am indebted to Elizabeth Pamba and Charles Kamande, my long-time research contacts at Starehe Boys Centre and School, without whose support this work would not have been completed nor gained its current depth and shape. I also thank John Ambani, formerly of Kenya National Archives, who provided numerous archival research information on Wamumu and Manyani detention camps and youth clubs that was a precious mine of vital information about the dates and activities discussed in this book. Additionally, my special gratitude goes to series editors John Rury and William Reese for reading several drafts of the manuscript with rigor and diligence, and for making insightful suggestions for improving the book. Finally, I am grateful to all interviewees who participated in the project; and, as always, my family, for their constant love, understanding, and support in all my academic engagements over the years.

Contents

1 Early Life and Entry in Kenyan Youth Education   1

2 The University of Hard Knocks: Manyani Detention Camp   23

3 A Place of Hope: Wamumu Rehabilitation Camp ("Eton of Africa")   45

4 Called to Educate: Kariokor and Starehe Youth Clubs   79

5 A Flower in the Mud: The Founding of Starehe Boys Centre and School and Its Growth   119

6 Conclusion: Thoughts on Youth Education and School Leadership   169

References   183

Index   187

List of Figures

Fig. 3.1   Captain George Gardner, officer in-charge of Wamumu (Photo by author from Starehe School archives)   47
Fig. 3.2   Wamumu Rehabilitation Camp entrance gate (Photo by author from Starehe School archives)   49
Fig. 3.3   Youths at Wamumu ready to participate in daily activities (Photo by author from Starehe School archives)   49
Fig. 3.4   Youths participating in physical education at Wamumu (Photo by author from Starehe School archives)   50

Fig. 4.1   Kariokor youth club (Photo by author from Starehe School archives)   111
Fig. 4.2   Starehe youth club (Photo by author from Starehe School archives)   112
Fig. 4.3   Boys who joined Starehe and Kariokor youth clubs at an early stage (Photo by author from Starehe School archives)   113

Fig. 5.1   Two tin huts where Starehe Boys Centre and School begun (Photo by author from Starehe School archives)   125
Fig. 5.2   Geoffrey Griffin and two boys, Peter Njenga and George Waigwa of Starehe Boys Centre and School in London 1962, as part of youth help campaign to raise funds for the school (Photo by author from Starehe School archives)   126
Fig. 5.3   Geoffrey Griffin and two boys, Peter Njenga and George Waigwa, of Starehe Boys Centre and School in London in 1962, on the terrace of the House of Commons with two Members of Parliament, as part of the Youth Help Campaign to raise funds for the school (Photo by author from Starehe School archives)   127

xv

xvi LIST OF FIGURES

Fig. 5.4	Cofounders of Starehe Boys Centre and School: Geoffrey Geturo, Joseph Gikubu, and Geoffrey Griffin (Photo by author from Starehe School archives)	128
Fig. 5.5	Opening of Starehe Boys Centre and School (Photo by author from Starehe School archives)	129
Fig. 5.6	Geoffrey Griffin at an early recruitment rally to encourage youths to join Starehe and Kariokor youth clubs (Photo by author from Starehe School archives)	130
Fig. 5.7	Joseph Gikubu and Geoffrey Griffin in the early days of Starehe Boys Centre and School (Photo by author from Starehe School archives)	131
Fig. 5.8	Starehe Boys Centre and School early classrooms, made of tin and corrugated iron (Photo by author from Starehe School archives)	133
Fig. 5.9	Starehe Boys Centre and School's early workshops for various trades (Photo by author from Starehe School archives)	134
Fig. 5.10	Starehe Boys Centre and School, built by Oxfam (Photo by author from Starehe School archives)	140
Fig. 5.11	A visit by Indira Gandhi to Starehe Boys Centre and School (Photo by author from Starehe School archives)	147
Fig. 5.12	The visit by Princess Anne to Starehe Boys Centre and School (Photo by author from Starehe School archives)	148
Fig. 5.13	A visit by Bishop Desmond Tutu to Starehe Boys Centre and School (Photo by author from Starehe School archives)	149

CHAPTER 1

Early Life and Entry in Kenyan Youth Education

INTRODUCTION

Since this book is grounded in biographical inquiry, it begins by discussing the vitality of biographies in educational research in order to comprehensively examine and understand Joseph Gikubu's contributions to Kenyan youth education. It provides a definition of educational biographies, then looks at their relevance. This chapter opens with a discussion of the methods used to gather historical evidence for the book and the format that each chapter takes. This is vital in enabling the reader to understand the in-depth research work that went into the book and the rationale behind its format.

The research for this book was undertaken using various methodological tools. It is the culmination of ten years of research that began during my doctoral studies in 2004 but was enhanced thereafter through extensive fieldwork. The historical evidence was collected from both primary and secondary sources. The primary sources represent material collected in the field. They include open-ended interviews with the Gikubu family, and faculty, support staff, students, and administrators both (former and present) of Starehe Boys Centre and School (SBC) who knew Joseph Gikubu. Further primary evidence is drawn from participant observation of the daily educational activities of SBC over several years. This entailed attending Sunday church services, daily assemblies, weekly Friday student forums, class visits, and more. In addition, archival and document analysis was conducted, regarding Gikubu's involvement in Kenyan youth education

© The Author(s) 2017
P.O. Ojiambo, *Kenyan Youth Education in Colonial and Post-Colonial Times*, Historical Studies in Education,
DOI 10.1007/978-3-319-59990-8_1

at Manyani, Wamumu, the Othaya Approved School, youth clubs, and SBC. Examination and analysis of various Gikubu letters, memos, school records, pictures, institutional artifacts, and videos were helpful in revealing the educational activities that took place at these institutions in the colonial and postcolonial periods, their purpose, related events, and Gikubu's involvement and role in them. This information enabled an assessment of much of the colonial literature and propaganda about the "colonial civilizing mission" of many of the educational programs that were undertaken in several of the institutions in which Gikubu worked. Other primary evidence collection methods included in-depth analysis of various audiovisual documentaries and interviews that were conducted with Gikubu concerning his involvement with and contributions to Kenyan youth education. Finally, a significant portion of information was drawn from various secondary sources. This formed the foundation of the study, and included the few available books, newspapers, and past studies that mentioned Gikubu. Together, the primary and secondary data enabled the development of an in-depth, critical, and comprehensive analysis of Gikubu's involvement with and contributions to Kenyan youth education in both the colonial and postcolonial periods.

Since this is an interpretive educational biography, the book does not focus on Gikubu per se as an individual or on the chronological flow of his life. Rather, it discusses his involvement and role in Kenyan youth education in light of its historical development in the colonial and postcolonial periods. To achieve this purpose, each chapter provides a detailed discussion and analysis of certain historical events that underpinned his involvement in this area, and interprets his involvement, role, and contributions in light of these and the government educational policies that guided them. In order to achieve this educational biographical focus, it proved necessary to place more emphasis on Gikubu's involvement with and contributions to Kenyan youth education than on his personal life, which would have made the book akin to a general biographical work. This approach therefore leaves room for Gikubu's biography.

The Relevance of Biographies in Educational Research

Educational biographies are increasingly becoming standard elements of qualitative research for both researchers and the general public.[1] A number of commentators have explored in depth the role of educational biographies in fostering educational inquiry. It is important to note, however, that although there has been a steady growth in general African biographies in the last decade, there have been few discipline-specific biographies, especially in the area of education. This is despite the common recognition on the African continent of the significant role that education and educators have played and continue to play in national development. It is this dearth of scholarship that this book addresses.

The last two decades have witnessed a growing interest in life writing, with various allusions and references to biographical works. Craig Kridel observes that this development has the potential to bridge critical relationships between the balkanized research realms that epitomize the study and importance of education. He opines:

> Good biographies deal with the way people faced living. They tell how they met problems, how they coped with big and little crises, how they loved, competed, did the things we all do daily. They touch familiar chords in readers. They help in understanding how and why something transpired. They illuminate action and reveal meaning.[2]

Biographies are seen as vital in expanding human relations. They encourage the crossing of boundaries, and "by reading biographies, written and lived stories often we connect and we realize we are not alone, we can live with another human being in another age, we can identify with his journey through the vicissitudes of life and its various gifts and challenges."[3] Beyond their capacity to reveal the origin of ideas and the existence of social possibilities and alternatives, biographies are also seen as providing a space in which the nature of societal change and development can be observed.

Much contemporary writing in the field of education draws its findings from the vital fields of social sciences and concentrates mainly on issues of narrative, life history, storytelling, voice, and autobiography. Psychology, feminist studies, critical theory, anthropology, and sociology are all well represented, with minimal reference to the humanities. The insights that have emerged from these varied fields and from current postmodern sensibilities have impacted the scholarly conceptualization of educational research and its influence on other fields. It is vital to note that educational biographies draw their writing structures from all disciplines and are therefore complex research approaches to the wide subject structures they draw on. Their analytical processes are also multifaceted.

Although dimensions of narrative and life history writing are pervading qualitative research, a significant body of literature in the growing field of biographical theory seems to have affected educational discourse. Much of this work is overlooked in the academy. Although distinctions between various types of life writing are often intricate, complex, and sometimes confusing, a distinct tradition of biography exists that can be critically examined. This body of work points towards the need for further inquiry into the field of education, as a way of reexamining educational research methods in relation to current postmodernist trends and thoughts. It is in this respect that biographical research presents new prospects, possibilities, and dimensions for educational inquiry and thought. It provides new pathways for examining the effects of the pedagogical process on students, educators, policymakers, and the overall teaching and learning process. In addition, it helps to explain how education policy manifests itself in the lives of individuals and their role in shaping and being shaped by it.

Even though there are already various collections of biographical studies, which connote a growing interest in educational biography, they do not provide a coherent discourse about or exploration of how the approach can be effectively utilized in educational research or its overall benefits in the field of education. This calls for more research in order to interpret various facets and advantages of biography in the context of educational research and thought. Looking at individual educators and their role in the development of education is thus a good entry point when addressing the complexities of biography and its utilization in the educational field, as well as how education can help the societal reconstruction process.

From the current literature on biographies, it can be deduced that biography is a rapidly growing qualitative form of study that requires further inquiry, especially when it is examined through varied discipline frames. This book is therefore significant in contributing further to this rapidly evolving area. It endeavors to show why Joseph Gikubu became involved in Kenyan youth education, the circumstances that necessitated his involvement, and his contribution to the subject. It examines the actions he undertook when addressing Kenyan youth education challenges, in both the colonial and postcolonial periods. It sheds light on his insights into youth education and educational leadership. This is the central aim of biographies: "they help us to understand how and why something transpired, they illuminate action and reveal meaning."[4] It is this that Ngugi wa Thiong'o alludes to in *Moving the Centre* when he writes about the significance of Nelson Mandela in South Africa's liberation struggle. He states:

All these figures are heroic because they reflect more intensely in their individual souls, the souls of their community. Their uniqueness is the uniqueness of the historical moment. They make history even as history makes them. They are torches that blaze out new paths. Mandela has been such a torch for the South African people. The black people of South Africa are reflected in Mandela. In Mandela, the people of the world have really been applauding the courage, the endurance, the resistance, and the spirit of the South African masses. The people of the world, particularly Africans and those of African descent outside Africa, have in turn seen themselves reflected in the struggling South African masses. Mandela is to black South Africa's struggles what black South Africa's struggles are to the democratic forces of the world in the twentieth century. Indeed, South Africa is a mirror of the modern world in its emergence over the last four hundred years.[5]

Biographies Critiqued

Since this work is an educational biography that examines contemporary historical aspects, it takes note of the general criticisms made of biographical works: some scholars view biography as an insignificant and unworthy branch of scholarship, irrespective of the discipline that uses it. From a general perspective, they view it as tending to promote the cult of the individual in the historical process and making heroes of historically insignificant individuals. Biographies are seen as an attempt to enhance the so-called "big man" theory at the expense of a well-balanced understanding of a people's political, historical, cultural, and economic life.

Contemporary biographies can be more problematic, complex, and intricate especially if the subject of the study is still alive. This is because the critical challenge a biographer faces is the passing of premature judgment on the person about whom he is writing. According to Ezekiel Adeoti, "the subject of the researcher is seen as still being on the stage and until the curtain falls, any judgment one may pass can only be tentative."[6] He attributes this to the existence of records that are not within the reach of the researcher. Affirming this, Edwin Mba notes that it is difficult to probe deeply if the subject is still alive; the tendency of interviewees to conceal or misconstrue information, whether deliberately or unconsciously, is hard to suppress.[7] He argues that passions and prejudices buzz around any living subject, and that a researcher has to contend with this, particularly when the biographical subject is an active agent of change and is still involved in various activities. The study discussed here takes this critique into consideration, since the fieldwork was conducted when Gikubu was alive and was actively engaged in the management of SBC. The study utilized several archival works and other triangulation methods to probe certain areas and to ascertain the validity of certain information.

Despite the negative attitudes reported above, biography has not been totally rejected as a reputable branch of qualitative inquiry. According to Craig Kridel, biographies are seen as empowering and having many societal benefits. He writes that "biography, especially of the great and good who have risen by their own exertions to eminence and usefulness, is an inspiring and ennobling study and has enormous benefits to society."[8] Every biography, according to Francis Coker, entails a scrutiny of the past, and makes observations that may be relevant to society in the future. Biographical study has led to an in-depth understanding of the complex and fluid historical, social, political, and economic contexts under which the subject functioned.[9] It is this purpose that this book strives to achieve. It seeks to verify Jacob Ajayi's argument that some biographies can rise above the mere provision of source material and become important essays in their own right, which interpret and analyze complex societal events.[10]

It is essential to note that although there are numerous works on the development of education in Kenya, few of them address the role that specific educators have played in its growth. Apart from the works of Kennedy Hongo and Jesse Mugambi, Roger Martin and Joseph King'ala, which mention Gikubu in some ways with regard to SBC, limited attempts have been made to examine his contributions to Kenyan youth education.

EARLY YEARS AND SCHOOLING

Joseph Gikubu was born in Banana Hill, Kiambu County, in 1934. He was the fourth child in a family of seven and the second among sons in his mother's household. His father Gikubu Karanja was a polygamous man who had five wives and 20 children. Gikubu's mother, Serah Wanjiku, was the third wife. His father initially worked with the police as a sergeant for 25 years and then took to small-scale livestock farming in several parts of Nairobi. His mother was a farmer and a small trader of farm produce. Gikubu grew up as a rural boy, running daily chores that his parents assigned him. He was always fascinated by rural life and its numerous adventures.

Gikubu's early childhood was marked by much engagement in various family economic and social activities. It was a very close family. Reflecting on their upbringing and the influence of their parents, Gikubu's sister Gladys Wambui observed that "we grew up as a very close family. Our parents imbibed in us values of education, hard work, the importance of love, respect, family unity, and helping needy persons. We have tried to ensure that these ties and values are maintained in our children."[11]

Gikubu went to Muchatha, Kanunga, and Riara schools between 1945 and 1950. He had a strong desire to get a good education. Although small in stature and age, he was intelligent at school and performed well in various subjects. Because of his brilliance at school, many of his classmates frequently sought his counsel on different subjects. Gikubu's schooling was interrupted when he was in grade eight owing to the declaration of the State of Emergency in 1952 and his active participation in Kenya's independence struggle movement (Mau Mau). Because of the heavy workload that was entailed in the movement's work, it became apparent to Gikubu that balancing his school work and the movement's activities was going to be a daunting task. He decided to quit school at the age of 15 to concentrate fully on Mau Mau activities. This decision marked his entry into Kenyan youth education at an early age. Gikubu's work entailed traveling throughout Kenya, drafting, training, and sensitizing youth on the movement's aims. His involvement in the Mau Mau movement, and its effects and influence on his life and entry into youth education, are discussed later in this chapter.

Gikubu married Gladys Mary Nduta in 1960 and together they had seven children: two boys and five daughters. As a parent, he was always involved in the education of his children. Recalling his emphasis that they should excel in school, his daughter Jacky Gikubu noted that "my father was very much involved in our studies. He constantly urged us to do well in school. He also emphasized to us the importance of mentoring the youth and helping the poor in society."[12] It was clear even to his family that Gikubu had a passion for youth education.

Further Schooling and Professional Training

In 1955 Gikubu undertook several trade courses at Wamumu Rehabilitation Camp in carpentry, masonry, and physical training. After Kenya's independence, while working at SBC, he received further high school education at New Trier High School, Winnetka, Illinois, between January 10, 1964 and June 28, 1966, but had to terminate his studies despite good progress in order to tend to his young family, as evidenced in this communication from his sponsor, Reynold Hillenbrand of Sacred Heart Church, to the management of SBC. He wrote:

I asked Joseph Gikubu to return because as a priest, I felt he could no longer be away from his young children and his wife. Joseph's conduct has been exemplary. New Trier High School, Winnetka, took a special interest in him and wished him to stay and complete his course. I saw at first hand his intense industriousness and interest in his studies. Fortunately, New Trier High School arranged that he can finish his high school course and receive a diploma through a correspondence course at the University of Nebraska. We have paid the initial fee for this and will pay the other fees. I am reluctant to see Joseph go, whom I hold in high regard, but a family especially with very young children is the paramount consideration. I am grateful for all you have done for him.[13]

Gikubu received further training in social welfare from Western Reserve University between April and August 1962 and later at Cleveland University in 1967 in youth leadership. Additionally, he visited Christ's Hospital School in England between May and June 1977 to study its structure, administration, and academic standards. The school was chosen because, like SBC, it is a public school that caters for students from less privileged socio-economic backgrounds. Gikubu learnt many approaches to effective school management from his visit, as indicated in this communication from Geoffrey Griffin to the management of Christ's Hospital School after Gikubu's return:

> Joseph Gikubu has returned to us in excellent state. Besides briefing me, he has already talked about his experience to the school in full assembly and, at greater length, to a meeting of school prefects. Later this week, he will spend an hour in question and answer session with our *"Baraza"* (school parliament). So his newly-gained knowledge of your traditions is being widely disseminated in our community. I am certain that the things that Joseph learned, will be of very much benefit to Starehe. Kindly, convey to the council my warm appreciation of its generosity in this matter. We are grateful for all your help.[14]

It was this modest education, professional training, and experience that Gikubu utilized at the various institutions he worked in for more than five decades, in order to equip Kenyan youth with the values, skills, and knowledge that would make them productive members of society.

THE MAU MAU WAR AND HOW IT SHAPED GIKUBU'S ENTRY INTO KENYAN YOUTH EDUCATION

Gikubu's involvement in Kenyan youth education was a serendipitous process that was influenced by various forces. First and foremost, his entry into it was shaped by the events of the Mau Mau War and its aftermath, especially the detention and rehabilitation programs that were instituted to address the plight of youth who were involved in the war. This was after the Mau Mau movement had shown its hand with the killing of Senior Chief Waruhiu, who was well known for his loyalty to the colonial government. Waruhiu had stood out firmly against the Mau Mau movement, and had tried to convince the Kikuyu community that an oath taken in secret and under duress had no binding force and power on them. After attending his funeral the following day, the Kenyan governor, Sir Evelyn Baring, cabled London to request State of Emergency powers. The following morning, he launched Operation Jock Scott and declared a State of Emergency. The stage was set for the final, conclusive struggle which was to lead to Kenya's independence. Baring managed to prevent all the final preparations for a revolt and was able to organize the arrest of all the suspected Mau Mau leaders, the operation being directed against more than 180 of them. Caroline Elkins writes:

> In the early morning of October 21, 1952 scores of Kenyan policemen, White and Black zealously carried out their arrest orders, rousing suspected Mau Mau protagonists like Paul Ngei, Fred Kubai, and Bildad Kaggia, handcuffing them, and hauling them off to Nairobi police station. Operation Jock Scott ushered in the colony's rapid decline. Contrary to official wisdom, Mau Mau did not collapse with the arrest of the politicals but instead turned more violent as the movement's leadership passed into the hands of younger men, the same men who for months had been pushing Kenyatta and others to adopt a more radical course.[15]

The State of Emergency approach was borrowed by Baring from the Federation of Malaya, which had been under a State of Emergency since 1948 and provided Baring and his ministers with a blueprint for emergency regulations. This had a major influence on the shape and direction of the Mau Mau rehabilitation program that evolved in Kenya in 1953, one of its victims being Gikubu. The colonial government feared that if the situation persisted Africans were likely to put up heavy resistance, which could destabilize colonial rule. Nobody knew what was likely to happen if war was to erupt. There were numerous rumors and anxiety among both Africans and whites. After a while, the colonial government discovered that it was dealing with a guerrilla war, and there were signs that it could escalate if not nipped in the bud. What began as a small group of disgruntled Kikuyus grew in size and might, and as the numbers increased so did the resultant fear, destruction of property, and loss of human life. Geoffrey Griffin recalled:

> It begun very slowly. It was noticeable that guns were disappearing from homes, hotel rooms, under very strange circumstances. Then some murders begun. The one that sticks in mind is the Ruck murders, where they attacked a homestead up on the other side of the Kinangop and murdered the man, his wife and a little boy. These things were beginning to escalate and it was obvious something big was just about to burst and the government of course woke up to it and declared a State of Emergency.[16]

European settlers complained bitterly, but the colonial government took its time. It had underrated the Kikuyus. According to Kennedy Hongo and Jesse Mugambi, government officials asked, "how could the Kikuyus fight? They are just miserable whining house servants! Now if they had been the Maasai, we would be worried."[17] With this mindset, young European men prowled about with their guns at the ready, trigger-happy and dreaming vainly of pitched battles with legions of spear-hurling warriors, confident that in a show of strength on their part they would quickly douse the Africans' immature political aspirations. There was a general feeling in the colonial government that the Mau Mau fighters would be overrun and neutralized within a very short time, but with time the government realized that it was dealing with a smart and determined force. It had underestimated the resolve and the ingenuity of the Mau Mau movement, and had forgotten how many Africans had acquitted themselves well in active service during the two world wars. They had no conception that guerrilla warfare was to be waged in their midst, dragging on for years. Describing the situation, Caroline Elkins states:

> In late October in 1952, on the farming plateau above Naivasha the disemboweled corpse of Eric Bowker, a settler and veteran of both world wars, was found in his home. Less than a month later, an elderly couple living at the edge of the Aberdares forest, near Thompson Falls, were sitting down for their coffee after dinner when they were attacked by Mau Mau guerrillas.

The husband, a retired naval commander Ian "Jock" Meiklejohn, collapsed while loading his shot-gun and died two days later. His wife, a retired doctor, survived despite extensive mutilation of her torso and breasts. Four days later Tom Mbotela's body was found in a muddy pool of water near Burma Market in Nairobi. An outspoken critic of Mau Mau movement and an African-appointed member of the City Council, Mbotela was reviled by many Africans. That evening the Burma Market was burned to the ground by the local police, infuriated by Mbotela's death and the defiant indifference of the locals. On a farm not far from where Eric Bowker had been murdered, the Ruck family was hacked to death by their trusted servants.[18]

Because of these atrocities, the settler community demanded quick summary justice and the elimination of the Mau Mau movement by any means necessary. In their memoranda to Michael Blundell, a leading politician and a member of the Kenya Legislative Council, they urged him to put troops into Kikuyu villages and to shoot 50,000 villagers—men, women, and children. Local Europeans castigated the colonial government, and Governor Baring in particular, for failing to eliminate the Mau Mau movement, and "many called for a wholesale extermination of the Kikuyu population."[19] Owing to the heinous atrocities and the scale of the war, the colonial government decided to mobilize a military force to handle the Mau Mau fighters. As part of this, young European men were sent for military training in Zimbabwe. Among the Mau Mau fighters in both the forests of Central Province and the alleys of Nairobi were youths under the age of 16, and it was this group that Gikubu had joined earlier on as a youth leader while in junior school. He helped the Mau Mau movement to spread its tenets and also assisted in the administration of oaths for its new members.

The declaration of the State of Emergency and the colonial government's efforts to suppress the Mau Mau movement's activities halted the colonial juvenile policy reforms that were in place by the late 1940s. Changing perceptions towards African youth, and the appropriate methods of controlling them within the colonial administrative structure, arose. In order to understand Gikubu's involvement in the Mau Mau movement, youth activities, and the independence struggle during this period, it is imperative to understand the colonial youth policies that were in place at the time. During the initial years of the State of Emergency, colonial government policies regarding African youth were hostile, unclear, and in most cases involved their periodic arrests, removals, and repatriations on an unprecedented scale, a process of which Gikubu became a victim.

COLONIAL GOVERNMENT POLICIES FOR HANDLING YOUTH VAGRANCY

Owing to the Mau Mau War, and the subsequent declaration of the State of Emergency in 1952, African family social networks, which had begun to be destroyed with the onset of colonization, were adversely weakened, and some were completely eliminated. The battle between the Mau Mau movement and the colonial state, according to Paul Ocobock, was played out in the forests of Central Province as well as on the streets of Nairobi. The military campaign in the forest resulted in a mass influx of Kikuyus into Nairobi to escape the conflict. Colonial officials realized later that some citizens of Nairobi were an integral part of the Mau Mau movement.[20] To meet the challenge in the capital city, Governor Baring's government relied on a series of regulations that affected the people of Central Province and, most significantly, Nairobi. The State of Emergency's movement of the Kikuyus and the control of Kikuyu labor regulations that were gazetted in 1952 provided the state with the power to forcibly remove suspected Mau Mau followers and their sympathizers from Nairobi. Armed with these powers, police and military forces began to encircle African townships and round up suspected Mau Mau sympathizers, repatriating them to their reserves. Many of those arrested were unemployed, of the sort normally arrested for vagrancy and pass law offenses. The government repatriated most of the Kikuyu population living outside the reserves to African landholdings and confined tens of thousands of suspected Mau Mau operatives in a series of detention camps. Through a network of transit camps, the state was able to filter through the Kikuyus who were captured and returned to the reserves, separating the hardline fighters from passive sympathizers. The ineffective policy of repatriation, the primary vehicle of removing vagrants from Nairobi, became key to rooting out Mau Mau followers and destroying much of the movement's networks and activities.[21]

Operation Anvil took removal and repatriation to an unparalleled level. On April 23, 1954, Nairobi was surrounded by military and police forces, and over the course of the next three weeks 50,000 Africans were interrogated. By the end of Operation Anvil, some 4,000 children had been repatriated back to their homes; and in 1956 another 3,000 had been removed to Kiambu.[22] Operation Anvil had the effect of cutting off Mau Mau operations in the forest from the supplies that were obtained in Nairobi, and severely damaged the Mau Mau ability to sustain and enlarge the conflict. The operation and intensification of the state's repatriation and screening processes had devastating and profound effects on youth and on the Mau Mau movement in general. Any young person rounded up by the police, whether a vagrant, suspected criminal, or someone who was simply in the wrong place at the wrong time, could be sent through the repatriation program. No rules outlawed the presence of African juveniles in the detention camps, but it was illegal for them to be sentenced to detention camps for Mau Mau-related offenses and activities.[23] Despite this legal clause, the administration was incarcerating youths under the age of 16 in great numbers in detention facilities on suspicion of being Mau Mau operatives or for engaging in the movement's activities, as illustrated by this report:

> Youth of fifteen years of age and upwards were enrolled in forest gangs. Many took part in actions, and some rose to hold rank in spite of their youth. By August 1955, there were some 1,200 youth in detention for Emergency offences. Children under the age of fourteen were being charged with Mau Mau offences, and those as young as four years old were found in the detention camps without any noticeable parent or guardian.[24]

The youth who escaped detention or returned home, particularly in the year following Operation Anvil, found rural areas radically changed. While Operation Anvil had cut off the Mau Mau movement from supplies in Nairobi, the process of villagization served a similar function in rural areas. By October 1955, the government had constructed 854 villages in Central Province and forcibly moved in 1,077,500 Kikuyus, Merus, and Embus. The state hoped to exercise greater control over the Kikuyus in these villages. Armed guards posted around the perimeter walls kept Mau Mau rebels out and sympathizers in. Life in the villages was far from ideal for the youth. With most of the men being detained while their loyalties were investigated, the new villages were primarily run by women who were left to manage the domestic households.[25] Visitors bemoaned that the places were occupied solely by children, most of whom were complaining of various illnesses. They were witnessing firsthand the gutting of Kikuyu society. It was no wonder that as late as 1959 officials complained that "villagization had merely exacerbated the rural-to-urban migration of the youth and had produced its own problems of dangerous youth gangs."[26] However, despite the stringent State of Emergency regulations, Operation Anvil, and villagization operations, Kikuyus and other African youths were not kept out of Nairobi for the remainder of 1956. This massive repatriation scheme suffered the same ineffective fate as its more modest predecessors. It simply repatriated juveniles out of the city, and they returned within a year. Operation Anvil and villagization policies offered little respite for European urbanites in Nairobi; juvenile vagrancy continued to plague the city, and soon crime began to rise.[27]

Operation Anvil was successful, though, in cutting off Mau Mau fighters in the forests of Central Province from their Nairobi supply lines, and for the first time in the city's history nearly all homeless and jobless vagrants were removed and repatriated, albeit temporarily. Although it was a turning point in the war, Operation Anvil did little to prevent the return of citizens, particularly the youth, to Nairobi. The state failed to provide a permanent solution to youth urban migration, or provide improved housing, education, and employment. Instead, the colonial administration quickly discovered that its massive repatriation and detention policies had created a population of parentless, rootless, crime-prone, and non-educated juveniles. As the social and economic processes that resulted in urban migration continued unchecked, the state was confronted with two separate populations of African youth between which the lines of distinction were slim and intricate. On one hand, administrators held a small number of youth suspected of Mau Mau support or criminal activities in Nairobi, and on the other there was a much greater number whose parents were detained or dead, and therefore had no home to which they could return.

By 1955, with the levels of juvenile crime and vagrancy on the increase, new measures were required to effectively manage youth during the emergency. In an improvised fashion characteristic of juvenile vagrancy policy of the 1940s, the state constructed a separate system to manage the children of the Mau Mau in accordance with the Emergency Welfare of Children Regulation Act of 1955. This provided district commissioners with the authority to round up any African youth whose parents were prevented from looking after them because they were imprisoned, detained, or incapacitated owing to the State of Emergency. These youths were subsequently placed in so-called "approved institutions." For those accused of vagrancy, criminal acts, or participation in the Mau Mau War, there was no longer any room for them in the approved schools and remand homes in the Nairobi penal system. As a result, officials incarcerated them in specialized youth camps, which were intended to cleanse them of their Mau Mau ideology and practice. For others, juvenile reception centers and youth clubs were established to bring order to repatriation and to stymie the movement of youth back to urban centers. By late 1955, this system pieced together refurbished, preexisting mechanisms such as approved schools and repatriation with new institutions that would detain juveniles, prevent their return to urban life, and reintroduce them to the tenets of Western society.[28] Although the early years of conflict had stifled developments in juvenile policies during the late 1940s, the later years of the State of Emergency rejuvenated them. Notions of citizenship, modernity, and the transformation of unproductive youth into disciplined and hardworking members of society came back into operation. Behind the barbed wire fences, a new relationship between state and youth took place, one that served to camouflage the continued failure of the state over the years to address the root causes of juvenile vagrancy.

The colonial government's lack of a comprehensive policy for handling youth vagrancy and education had tremendous effects on those who lacked adequate social safety valves to address their numerous problems. During this period, thousands of young people were engaging in vagrant activities, and there were no adequate government programs in place to address their plight. Commenting on the precarious situation of youth during this period and the role SBC played in alleviating the problem, Roger Martin writes:

> Until the Starehe and Kariokor youth clubs opened their doors, there was almost no attempt made to care for the hordes of children living on the streets of Nairobi. A church club at Karen met one evening a week, another in Pumwani on two evenings. The Christian Industrial Training Centre in Pumwani offered a full-time training course, but only for those who had reached Standard Seven in primary school, and furthermore on a fee-paying basis. The Save the Children Fund home at Ujana Park had closed early in 1958. There was virtually nothing else. All that a boy could look forward to was periodic arrest, judicial beating, perhaps repatriation to his home area, where he would be unwelcome and from which he would promptly return to Nairobi; and, eventually, an approved school or prison. The city authorities showed little enthusiasm for clubs.[29]

The effects of the Mau Mau War further aggravated the desolate state of youth during this period. Teenagers took to roaming the countryside in gangs: they indulged in petty thefts, malicious damages to farms, and, in some cases, smoked bhang. During the war, thousands of men, most of them heads of families, were arrested and held in detention camps; others lost their lives through their refusal to support the Mau Mau movement. In the Kikuyu reserves, countless families lost their identities when forced to move into temporary fortified villages. Traditional customs and loyalties,

16　1　EARLY LIFE AND ENTRY IN KENYAN YOUTH EDUCATION

sorely beset by colonial rule, disintegrated still further under the intolerable pressures of the time; and more and more children, especially boys, found themselves without the support of parents and family. There was no refuge in the country for these homeless youths. Even the youngest were caught up in the inevitable trek to Nairobi, the distant, glamorous city where they hoped for a better life. The realities of life in Nairobi for destitute children were bitterly difficult, uncertain, and agonizing. Anxious parents, administrative systems, and police officers could do very little to address the problem of youth vagrancy, given the lack of clear colonial government policies. To worsen the situation, schools could not provide answers for the young delinquents. Describing the education quagmire during this period, Geoffrey Griffin observes that:

> In February 1962, the Ministry of Education reported a primary school enrolment of 653,000 children, aged between 7 to 10 years. It was estimated that 119,000 children in this age bracket were out of school. In the intermediate range between the ages of 11 to 14 years, 228,000 children were in school and about 438,000 were not! Of the estimated 600,000 children between 15 to 18 years, only a small percentage was in high schools![30]

The colonial approaches to solving youth vagrancy were adapted from British youth vagrancy models in order to suit the needs of Nairobi's city demographics. The presence of an economic and socially insecure population of white expatriates proved irksome to many colonial officials. Although colonial Nairobi differed from London in many ways, youth vagrancy still operated at the epicenter, where labor crisis and urban order converged. It was this core continuity that ultimately governed the development of colonial youth vagrancy policies in Kenya. However, colonial ideas of gender, age, and race, as well as the economic constraints of the colonial system and settler anxieties, were but some of the factors that gave Kenyan youth vagrancy a unique identity. The situation was complex and demanded comprehensive local solutions and approaches.

Inadequate colonial youth policies during this period accelerated the number of youth vagrants in Nairobi. The colonial state lacked the resources to enforce firmer social control or to enhance social provisions and engagement. Instead, it vacillated between imprisonment, corporal punishment, repatriation, and discharge. The colonial government's good intentions inevitably and invariably confronted the parsimony of government expenditure. Ordinances, legislative debates, and committee deliberations expressed concern and determination to tackle the problem of urban youth, but the colonial state lacked the necessary capacity, strategies, and finances to act effectively. Roundups and repatriation were seen as less costly than social programs and urban reforms. Despite the lofty designs of colonial legislation, vagrancy laws were merely a narrow-minded strategy to provide a semblance of order, so as to quell the fears of European and Asian urbanites about the dangers of increased levels of youth vagrancy. Indeed, the young vagrant was not alone in being trapped between the economic and political inadequacies of rural and urban environments. The state, too, was circumscribed by similar forces, incapable of managing the complexities of the youth problem it had created.[31] It was these increased levels of youth vagrancy that compelled Gikubu to join Geoffrey William Griffin and Geoffrey Gatama Geturo in the formation of youth clubs that eventually gave birth to SBC as a way of addressing the menace. His aim was to assist them in offering education to the youth who were trapped in these difficult circumstances. They purposed to provide a rich educational foundation that went beyond basic provisions of food, shelter, and clothing. According to Gikubu it was pointless to give them food and clothing without a sound education, which would provide them with tools that were vital to their navigation of the murky challenges that came to pass as a result of the Mau Mau War, racial colonial education, and youth vagrant policies. Like all those who were involved in the State of Emergency, Gikubu had witnessed brutality and atrocity committed by all parties. He longed to provide change and saw education as the sure route. The details of how this came to fruition are discussed in detail in Chaps. 4 and 5.

It was during Operation Anvil and the State of Emergency period that Gikubu was arrested in Banana Hill on suspicion of being a Mau Mau movement leader, and taken to Langata detention facility. Describing their journey to Langata, Gikubu noted:

> We were chased by Land Rovers, with a warning that if we did not run fast enough we would be run over. Upon our arrival at Langata we were received by tough guards who beat us up and took our money, watches and clothes. I was regarded as very dangerous person. I was placed in a separate underground sewer to prevent me from influencing other detainees. I stood there for four days with filthy water up to my knees. I was given very little food. I was fortunate enough to be restored to health by other detainees.[32]

Langata was a screening camp that served as a temporary destination for many of the Mau Mau suspects who were rounded up during Operation Anvil.

Britain's military forces, under the command of General George Erskine, launched an ambitious operation to reclaim full colonial control over Nairobi by purging the city of nearly all Kikuyus, Embus, and Merus living there. By the end of the operation, Britain's security forces had sent over 20,000 Mau Mau suspects for further screening at Langata camp and deported nearly 30,000 more back to the Kikuyu reserves. The only distraction in the nightmare of Langata was the loudspeaker system. From time to time it blared out a series of names. These men would be taken away, but no one knew where, why, or for how long. When one evening after three months at Langata Gikubu's name sounded through the loudspeaker, he learnt the answer to one of these questions. His stay in Langata was over. He was transferred, via a new station that had been built on the railway line nearby, to Mackinnon Road Detention Camp and later Manyani Detention Camp. Initially designed to house no more than 20,000 detainees, by May 1954 there were over 24,000 Mau Mau suspects in the Langata, Manyani, and Mackinnon Road camps. New intakes were coming in daily, in lorries, buses, and in railroad freight cars. In addition, others were being shipped in from European settled areas and the Kikuyu reserves. By the end of 1954, the "British colonial government reported that the detainee population had risen to over fifty-two thousand-an increase of 2,500 per cent from the beginning of the year."[33] Describing their transfer from Langata to Mackinnon Road, Gikubu observed:

> One morning we were told to line up. A roll call was taken. We were inspected to ensure we were all there. We were each given a blanket and by that evening around 7 o'clock, we were placed in lorries and taken to Nyayo Stadium where there were several barbed wire trains waiting for us. We were placed inside these trains and given two European guards. Each train had about 10,000 detainees. The trains were only required to travel at night. This was to ensure that none of us escaped.[34]

The trains travelled the entire night through the wilderness. They arrived at Mackinnon Road in the morning. There the detainees were separated, with about 5,000 youths being placed in one compound. They were told by the commandant that they would soon be released and returned to their homes. The conditions were terrible. Gikubu noted:

The place was full of torture. We stayed under deplorable conditions. There were hundreds of White officers and *askaris* (African police) who kept shouting at us and beating us. They ordered us to take off our clothes, they searched us thoroughly and then gave us a pair of yellow shorts and a blanket. They placed all our clothes in one pile and burned them. I was not sure whether I was going to live.[35]

When the detainees would be released from Mackinnon Road was not known, and there were daily rumors in the camp. Gikubu observed: "there were rumors that we will never go back, we will die in custody, and we will be taken to the worst camps in the country."[36] The worst reputation was attributed to Manyani Detention Camp. After a year in Mackinnon Road, Gikubu was transferred there. This was his first stint in this camp. Every detainee was "screened" by the Special Branch, with a view to determining his future detention period—this being based on his commitment to the Mau Mau cause. To be classified as "white" meant that you were clean and had a good chance of being released early and repatriated to the Kikuyu reserves, while "greys" were considered more compliant oathtakers. The detainees in this category required further rehabilitation and were sent down the pipeline to ordinary work camps in their home districts. The "blacks" were doomed to permanent incarceration. They were seen as the hardcore activists, who were sent for softening up in special detention camps set up by the colonial government in various parts of the country. Given Gikubu's earlier active role in the Mau Mau movement, he would have undoubtedly been classified in the "blacks" category had it not been for his shrewdness. Somehow, between Langata and Manyani, his name changed. He was no longer Joseph Kamiru Gikubu, but was known as Njenga Mbuthia. This allowed him to emerge from the screening process in the "greys" category. He was held at Manyani for a few months and then released.

His release was short lived, however. The morning after he arrived home, he was called upon and commanded to get into a vehicle, in which there were four police officers. He was taken to the area chief's office, and informed that he had been rejected by his village. This was because when he was detained some of the people who had taken oath under him had surrendered and confessed that they were given an oath by him. His village feared that Gikubu's return would force them to join the Mau Mau movement. There were two options that the area chief was required to consider. Either he could release him and whatever happened to him was none of his concern. Alternatively, he could send him back to Manyani Detention Camp, where his security was granted. The chief chose the latter. Gikubu was sent to Manyani for the second time in early 1955. His experiences there and their influence on his involvement in youth education are discussed in detail in Chap. 2.

This chapter describes Gikubu's early life and schooling, and the circumstances that led to his involvement in Kenyan youth education—the Mau Mau War and its aftermath. It illustrates the role that African youth played in Kenya's independence struggle and the price they paid for this: forfeiting schooling, imprisonment, mistreatment, and death. The lack of clear colonial policies on African education in general and youth education in particular is explored, together with the colonial policies that were utilized to handle youth vagrancy. It is evident that minimal education was offered to African youth during the colonial period, a situation that led to increased levels of youth vagrancy, something that was exacerbated further when the Mau Mau War broke out. The various colonial experiments, such as detentions, rehabilitation programs, and youth clubs reflect the lack of coherent programs relating to youth education and vagrancy during this period. In order to understand Gikubu's early works in Kenyan youth education, it is important to examine his activities in some of the detention facilities that he was taken to during this period, especially Manyani and Wamumu—and this is the subject of the next chapter.

Notes

1. John Creswell, *Qualitative Inquiry and Research Design* (Thousand Oaks, CA: Sage Publications, 1998).
2. Craig Kridel, *Writing Educational Biography: Explorations in Qualitative Research* (New York: Garland Publishing, 1988), 19.
3. Kridel, *Writing Educational Biography: Explorations in Qualitative Research*, 25.
4. Ibid., 19.
5. Ngugi Wa Thiong'o, *Moving the Centre: The Struggles for Cultural Freedoms* (Oxford: James Currey Limited, 1993), 147.
6. Ezekiel Adeoti, *Alayande as Educationist 1948–1983: A Study of Alayande's Contribution to Education and Social Change* (Ibadan: Educational Books), xvii.
7. Edward Mba, *Ayo Rosiji: Man with Vision* (Ibadan: Spectrum Books Limited, 1990).

8. Kridel, *Writing Educational Biography: Explorations in Qualitative Research*, 60.
9. Adeoti, *Alayande as Educationist 1948–1983: A Study of Alayande's Contribution to Education and Social Change*.
10. Jacob Ajayi, *History and the Nation and Other Addresses* (Ibadan: Spectrum Books, 1990).
11. Interview, Gladys Wambui, August 18, 2012.
12. Interview, Jacky Gikubu, August 18, 2012.
13. A letter of July 2, 1966 from Reynold Hillenbrand, Gikubu's sponsor to Starehe Boys Centre and School, detailing why he allowed Gikubu to return to Kenya.
14. A letter from Geoffrey Griffin to the management of Christ Hospital School in Britain on June 22, 1977, thanking them on the training they had provided to Gikubu.
15. Caroline Elkins, *Imperial Reckoning: The Untold Story of Britain's Gulag in Kenya* (New York: Henry Holt and Company, 2005), 35.
16. Documentary Interview, Geoffrey Griffin, September 4, 2004.
17. Kennedy Hongo and Jesse Mugambi, *Starehe Boys Centre: School and Institute. The First Forty Years 1959–1999* (Nairobi: Acton Publishers, 2003), 38.
18. Elkins, *Imperial Reckoning: The Untold Story of Britain's Gulag in Kenya*, 38.
19. Ibid., 43.
20. Paul Ocobock, "Joy Rides for Juveniles: Vagrant Youth and Colonial Control in Nairobi, Kenya, 1901–1952," *Social History*, 31.1 (2006): 39–59.
21. Ocobock, "Joy Rides for Juveniles: Vagrant Youth and Colonial Control in Nairobi, Kenya, 1901–1952".
22. Ibid.
23. Ibid.
24. KNA/AB/16/19/1957 Report.
25. Peter Ojiambo, *Teaching Beyond Teaching: Geoffrey William Griffin and Starehe Boys Centre and School*. Saarbrucken, Germany: VDM Verlag, 2008.
26. Ocobock, "Joy Rides for Juveniles: Vagrant Youth and Colonial Control in Nairobi, Kenya", 8.
27. Ibid.
28. Ibid.
29. Roger Martin, *Anthem of Bugles: The Story of Starehe Boys Centre and School* (Nairobi: Heinemann Educational Books Ltd., 1978), 6.
30. Yusuf King'ala, *The Autobiography of Geoffrey William Griffin: Kenya's Champion Beggar* (Nairobi: Falcon Crest, 2005), 58.
31. Bruce Berman, *Control and Crisis in Colonial Kenya: The Dialectic of Domination* (London: James Currey, 1990).
32. Interview, Joseph Gikubu, September 1, 2013.

33. Elkins, *Imperial Reckoning: The Untold Story of Britain's Gulag in Kenya*, 131.
34. Interview, Joseph Gikubu, June 23, 2013.
35. Interview, Joseph Gikubu, August 17, 2013.
36. Interview, Joseph Gikubu, June 24, 2013.

CHAPTER 2

The University of Hard Knocks: Manyani Detention Camp

Gikubu's first direct involvement in Kenyan youth education can be traced to his activities at the Manyani Detention Camp. In order to understand his involvement in youth education there it is important to understand the historical events of the time: the Mau Mau War and the colonial policies that were enacted to fight it. Operation Anvil, discussed in Chap. 1, netted thousands of African youths whom colonial government officials felt were hard-line Mau Mau leaders, fighters, followers, and sympathizers. Several of these youths aged between 16 and 18 were placed in detention camps such as Manyani, where they were interrogated about their involvement with the Mau Mau movement. This was no solution to defeating the Mau Mau fighters, however. Many liberal colonial government officials, such as Thomas Garrett Askwith, felt that a true victory could only be gained through rehabilitating Kikuyu fighters and winning the hearts and minds of the general African population through social and economic programs. These were the recommendations of Hugh Fraser's committee that was set up in September 1953 to evaluate the situation and to recommend what could be done to defuse charges of British misrule in Kenya at the time. On the one hand, the colonial government was straining to maintain its benevolent image as the advocate and protector of African interests in Kenya and in its empire at large, while on the other it was justifying its need for absolute power under the State of Emergency regulations. In his report to the Colonial Office, Fraser advocated for rehabilitation, whose role was to civilize the Kikuyus and the larger African population. Through rehabilitation:

> The civilizing mission, Britain's raison d'être for colonizing the Kikuyu people, could be introduced to the masses of Mau Mau adherents. This strategy would offer social and economic change to those Kikuyus who confessed their oaths and then cooperated with colonial authorities in the detention camps, and eventually in the Emergency villages in the Kikuyu reserves. Rehabilitation would be the inducement needed to lure the Kikuyu away from Mau Mau savagery toward Western civilization.[1]

Rehabilitation was to become the heart of the colonial government's campaign for winning the hearts and minds of the Kikuyu and other African groups that were involved in the Mau Mau movement. It was one of the central counterinsurgency efforts that were undertaken and was to form one of the main civilian campaign tools. This would not be the first time the British government had undertaken a hearts-and minds campaign to reorient detainees toward a more Western way of thinking and living. During and after the Second World War the British had attempted to de-Nazify German prisoners of war in order to cleanse them of their fascist and anti-Semitic beliefs. At the same time the British undertook similar psychological campaigns throughout the empire as part of a larger effort to repress postwar and anticolonial uprisings in some of their colonies. These were experiments in disciplinary power aimed at forcing individuals to reject their own ideas and to adopt the purported superior beliefs of their captors.

Of all the British hearts and minds precedents, the one undertaken in colonial Malaya as noted in Chap. 1 influenced the Kenyan rehabilitation policies and program in profound ways. Governor Baring looked to Malaya, believing that its rehabilitation program was offering sound civic and social improvements in order to lure communist insurgents and their supporters back to the capitalist and "civilized" ways of the British colonizers. Although the extent of his belief in the principles of rehabilitation or liberal reform was not clear and might be questioned, what is evident from the literature is that he was aware that the ideals of liberal reform would soften the tactics that underscored the broader civilian counterinsurgency. The Malayan Federation's High Commissioner, General Sir Gerald Templer, agreed to instruct a Kenyan civil servant on his hearts and minds program. Earlier on, he had provided Baring and his ministers with a blueprint for the State of Emergency regulations. Fortunately, as in many other parts of the world during this postwar period, Kenya was witnessing the rise of men and women who had progressive and transformative thoughts about issues of social welfare, citizenship, and African advancement. Thomas Askwith belonged to this group. It was because of this that he was chosen by Governor Baring to lead the rehabilitation program. He was a talented and seasoned administrator in development and African matters—credible, experienced, and informed. Having arrived in the colony in 1936 as a member of the colonial service, he spent ten years in the district administration as an officer in the Kikuyu reserves before becoming a municipal native affairs officer for Nairobi. His work there changed the course of his career. He witnessed firsthand the lives of the African urban poor and observed socioeconomic conditions that were scrupulously ignored by most Europeans in the colony. For Askwith, the urban slums epitomized the racial inequality that existed in Kenya at the time. Comprehending and understanding the Mau Mau crisis and activities required a man who was well versed with the situation, informed, a deep thinker, and experienced on the African social, political, and economic conditions, and Askwith was the ideal choice for the position.

It is important to note that his belief in African advancement and the practice of racial inclusion found him marginalized within official colonial circles at various stages of his life and career. A number of his erstwhile colleagues felt he was too lenient when it came to African advocacy of equality, social justice, higher education, empowerment, and social progress. Rehabilitation presumed, of course, Britain's inherent moral superiority over the Kikuyu and Africans in general, something that Askwith never questioned nor doubted. The colonial government's assumption here was that out of the ashes of Mau Mau a reconstructed Kikuyu and broader African society would emerge, and with it the threat of any future Mau Mau uprising would be prevented. When the colonial government thought of introducing a hearts and minds campaign, Governor, Baring viewed this as the antithesis of physical violence and summary justice. British colonial violence, however, could and did take many forms; and rehabilitation was no less coercive than some of the brutish tactics that were employed in the screening operations by colonial agents. Governor Baring understood that detention alone could not solve the Mau Mau problem or general African demands in the long term. Therefore he directed Askwith to develop a more comprehensive rehabilitation system that would ultimately eliminate Mau Mau influence from Kikuyu minds and from the African population at large.

By the end of his short tour Askwith was observing various reform programs that were being utilized in Malaya's detention camps, rehabilitation centers, emergency villages, approved schools for young offenders, and prisons. Templer's staff briefed him on their efforts to achieve a lasting peace in Malaya through the reeducation and resettlement of the communist insurgents and their followers. Askwith's observations during the tour were critical in providing him with a map for similar Emergency policies in Kenya. Caroline Elkins notes that:

> According to his (Askwith's) rather idealized tour report, issued in August 1953, the detention camps in Malaya were regarded not as punitive institutions but as opportunities to alter the attitude of the communist sympathizers and reinstill confidence in the British colonial government. The administrative structure of Malaya's camps emphasized rehabilitation. Templer had created a temporary Detention Camps Department under the Ministry of Defence, which was completely separate from the Prisons Department. Askwith made careful description of this part of the Malayan system by noting that it would be wrong for detainees, who are convicts to be placed under the Prisons Department as this would detract the value of the rehabilitation process itself. He felt that the rules governing rehabilitation were quite different from those concerning convicts. Further, Askwith also saw immeasurable value in quality and training of the staff and positive interactions between the officers and detainees.[2]

It is vital to note that in Malaya the rehabilitation process went beyond the confines of the camps, which indicated to Askwith a commitment at the highest level of Britain's efforts in implementing its civilizing mission throughout the colony, and especially in those areas that were heavily affected by the State of Emergency. According to Askwith, colonial officials in Malaya looked as if they were embracing reform. They recognized that the rehabilitation process could not succeed on its own, unless concrete evidence was provided by the government that it could offer a better future than the one promised by the communists. The government's overriding purpose was to remove bitterness among the detainees and the general public, especially the poor, and to construct a better life for them by meeting their social, economic, and political needs.

Rehabilitation was one part of a comprehensive strategy for reconstructing and shaping Malayan society entirely. With the work in camps linked to rural development and social reform measures in the emergency villages, those who suffered from communist intimidation in the countryside needed relief, reform, and later reintegration in society. Moreover, the colonial government had to create future homes and employment opportunities for former detainees in Malaya. The captured hearts and minds of reformed communist insurgents could be lost if they were released into a hostile or impoverished society that did not meet their immediate economic and social needs.

Delighted by Askwith's report and his commitment to the ideals and tenets of rehabilitation, Governor Baring officially appointed him to be in charge of a Mau Mau psychological and civic reform program in October 1953. His appointment took place immediately after Hugh Fraser's visit to Kenya and the release of his report, which underscored the importance of rehabilitation in the colony. Following the report's recommendations, Askwith's title was expanded to Commissioner for Community Development and Rehabilitation, and his responsibilities were expanded likewise. For instance, "he found himself overseeing the hearts-and-minds campaign for some fifteen hundred persons already detained under Emergency regulations, nine thousand convicts imprisoned for Mau Mau offenses, the many ex-squatters, and persons returned to the reserves as a result of screening, together with the waverers normally domiciled in the reserves."[3] He was also made the principal of Jeanes School, Kenya's adult education institute for Africans, from which he was expected to promote concepts of comprehensive African development and societal change.

Upon his appointment, Askwith was asked to spearhead the entire colonial rehabilitation program in Kenya and to implement its policies and practice. It is vital to note that the wholesale adoption of the Malayan rehabilitation program in the Kenyan situation was problematic given the varied social, political, and economic conditions of the two countries. According to Askwith, Kenya's difficulties seemed more challenging in several ways:

> Malaya had the deportation option; more than half of its 30,000 detainees were repatriated to China and those who remained in the camps had softer Communist sympathies and were easy to convert to the Western way of thinking. Despite Nairobi's arguments to the contrary, Mau Mau adherents belonged to the territory and therefore could not be exiled from Kenya. Secondly, Askwith thought the re-absorption problem was more difficult in Kenya than it had been in Malaya. Already over 100,000 displaced Kikuyus who had been forcibly deported from their homes outside Kikuyuland and were returning to the overcrowded African reserves, the same places to which

rehabilitated detainees would later be returning upon release from Kenya's camps. Employment opportunities and more importantly expanded land holding opportunities would have to keep pace with the release of detainees. While job creation for Kenya's African population was challenging enough, the land issue was another story altogether. For the settler population, there was no land issue in Kenya. The colonial government supported the self-serving view that the Kikuyus had ample land for subsistence production. Finally, there were the oaths. Even for Askwith, a liberal who recognized the socio-economic context of Kikuyu unrest, the oath represented everything evil in Mau Mau. Mass detention provided a form of quarantine and treating the disease.[4]

It is noteworthy that Askwith's views on Kikuyu's discontentment and engagement in the Mau Mau War differed from those of the colonial government and nearly every other European in the colony. For him the grievances of the Kikuyus and other Africans were legitimate and not the result of some kind of mass psychosis or body and mind impairment or defect. In his internal reports he strongly advocated for juvenile and adult education, unemployment relief, adequate housing programs, increased or improved wages, social security provisions, and more opportunities for Africans to acquire land. Further, he underscored the negative effects of the color bar and the bitterness that this brought to many Africans in Kenya. He delivered his final rehabilitation report to Baring in October 1953:

> It was a blueprint for winning the war against Mau Mau using socioeconomic and civic reform rather than destructive means. The oath takers, behind the barbed wire of detention, would confess their Mau Mau oaths, and in return the colonial government would offer them many of the reforms that it had failed to deliver during the first half century of colonial rule. With Askwith's plan, detention would not be a punitive measure but an opportunity for British colonizers to introduce dramatic changes. Behind the barbed wire the Kikuyu would confess their oaths and walk towards redemption and progress. A recipe of paid physical labor, craft training, recreation, and civic and moral re-education would produce governable men and women.[5]

Interestingly, Askwith had penned this civics primer years earlier, and it was now slated for translation, mass distribution, and implementation behind the wire. The process of rehabilitation developed by the Ministry of Community Development was founded on three main tenets: the inculcation of discipline and a work ethic, education in employable skills to prepare for future employment and settlement, and finally, the relearning and restoration of moral values. Although not an individual step in the process of citizenship construction, religion provided the glue that bound these stages together and was a central part of the entire rehabilitation program. Through the implementation of the Christian work ethic, spiritual cleansing, and moral guidance, the Kikuyu and the larger African population that was involved in the Mau Mau movement would be freed from the Mau Mau influence and would denounce its teachings. The tenets were expected to create a governable and productive citizenry.

Because of the complex progression procedures that were entailed, the Kenyan colonial government under Askwith's leadership called the system of detention and rehabilitation the "pipeline," denoting a detainee's or Mau Mau adherent's progression from initial detention through various rehabilitation programs until ultimate release. In the adult Mau Mau pipeline, where youths such as Gikubu were sent owing to a lack of juvenile facilities, rehabilitation began within the detention camps: Manyani was one of the few that existed in the country at the time. The prerequisite before entering the rehabilitation course was complete confession and reversing of the Mau Mau oath, activities, and practices. This process began at the transit camps, where screening teams of Europeans and African loyalists placed Kikuyus into three main categories that determined their level of reeducation, rehabilitation, and eventual release—as mentioned in Chap. 1. For the 'whites', simple repatriation back to their home was sufficient. Those more suspect Kikuyu men and women who were labeled "grey" were consigned to reception centers or holding camps, and after further screening they were sentenced to work camps where, once they confessed their oaths, they spent their days performing voluntary paid labor on government projects while attending rehabilitation courses in the evenings. Using a recipe of paid labor, craft training, recreation, civic, and moral reeducation, colonial officials expected to pacify the Mau Mau threat and produce a generation of governable African men and women. The more governable the "greys" became, the closer to home they were moved, until ultimately they were released by their district commissioners to their respective villages and homes in open camps. There, rehabilitation continued with instruction by local chiefs and headmen, who decided when a detainee's final release would take place. The "blacks," the recalcitrant Mau Mau fighters, the hardcore, the political hard cases, and those who were considered beyond redemption, were incarcerated in "permanent exile settlements," or special camps where they could be isolated from a society which was in the process of reconstruction and reform. It is important to note that even before the appointment of Askwith, Baring had ordered the construction of permanent exile settlements in various parts of Kenya to handle those detainees who were viewed as irreconcilable.

It is important to note that according to Askwith rehabilitation was as much about communal reform as it was about individual change. The dependents and relatives of detainees needed similar opportunities for social and civic change if the Kikuyu and African society at large was to experience a social counterrevolution. To achieve this, Askwith emphasized the need to cleanse both men and women, and especially the latter. He opined that it was vital to cleanse women before their men were permitted to rejoin them. He argued that there was evidence that in many cases wives persuaded their husbands to take the oath and were often very militant. They were also seen to be bringing up their children to follow the Mau Mau creed and practices. Askwith argued that it was important to rehabilitate the women rather than the men if the next generation was to be saved. To achieve this, the colonial government zeroed in on Kikuyu women and children with a plan to pursue a dogmatic program to break their allegiance to the Mau Mau movement. Community development and probation staff were to go to the reserves to oversee the rehabilitation of the Kikuyu family. There, they were expected to introduce communal confessions, or confessional meetings, to purge the women of their Mau Mau indoctrination and provide them with homecraft, childcare, and agricultural classes that would improve their lives. To Askwith, it was only through rehabilitation in the Kikuyu reserves that stability would take hold, that communal self-help would take off, and a multiracial future society would be realized. It is important to note that:

> Rehabilitation presumed Britain's inherent moral superiority over the Kikuyu, something Askwith never questioned. When they first thought of introducing a heart's- and-minds campaign, Baring and Lyttelton viewed it as the antithesis of physical violence and summary justice. British colonial violence, however, could and did take many forms, and rehabilitation was no less coercive than some of the brute-force tactics employed in screening operations by Britain's colonial agents. Nevertheless, on a relative scale rehabilitation was certainly much preferred to, say, the electric-shock torture, castration, or the other forms of physical brutality that were routinely used during interrogation.[6]

Despite knowing what was going on around him, Askwith's belief in rehabilitation was unshakable. He believed that out of the ashes of Mau

Mau a reconstructed Kikuyu and African society would arise, and with it the threat of any future uprising stymied. He had reason to believe that others, including Governor Baring, shared his vision of an impending social counterrevolution. It was for this reason that a month after he submitted his final rehabilitation report to Baring and Lyttelton, the colonial government endorsed it as official policy. Governor Baring made a public spectacle of his government's adoption of a hearts and minds campaign, advertising it in the newspapers in Kenya, Britain, and other parts of the world, with the help of his public relations offices in Nairobi and London.

During the State of Emergency period, there were thousands of youths being rounded up throughout Central Province, and while many were processed through the adult pipeline earlier discussed, most entered the juvenile pipeline. For the young Kikuyus captured during the fighting, rounded up in the rural areas, or removed by Operation Anvil from Nairobi, special youth camps were developed for their reeducation process and later reentry into society. The youth camp system was a government response to the State of Emergency as per the regulations of the Children Welfare Act of 1954.[7] As few nongovernmental organizations would take in suspected Mau Mau youths, the colonial regime needed to construct its own approved institutions to house the thousands of youths who were being detained owing to the stringent State of Emergency rules. Askwith and the Department of Community Development had come across the idea of youth camps four years earlier when an industrious officer from Machakos decided to solve the youth vagrancy problem in his area. He converted an abandoned labor center into a youth centre where a local artisan volunteered to provide courses in woodwork for former vagrant youths. The courses operated like an apprenticeship and the youths had to indenture themselves for two years to the program. The success of this pilot program led to more courses in blacksmithing and mechanics, and much later provided the backbone of the youth camp system.

Drawing on the program in Machakos, Askwith and his department developed their youth camps along the steps of the rehabilitation program earlier discussed. The first was established in 1954 at Gituyaini in Nyeri, and was deemed so successful that nine more were constructed in Fort Hall, Embu, and Meru districts. The camps originally served as holding sites for surrendered or suspected young Mau Mau followers, and they were not dismantled even after Mau Mau confrontations with the British forces subsided. The camps were transformed by the state from detention camps into rehabilitation camps during the State of Emergency. One of the largest youth camps of Central Province was located in Wamumu. It provided a fruitful demonstration of colonial rehabilitation and citizen-making at its most sincere and disturbing level, as will be evidenced in Chap. 3.

In the early years of the State of Emergency, the colonial government had not yet developed a coherent strategy to manage young people who were involved in or affected by the Mau Mau conflict. Prior to the State of Emergency, the colonial government did very little in response to its own internally generated recommendations regarding the need for juvenile delinquency facilities throughout the colony. With the notable exception of the approved schools for boys at Kabete and Dagoretti, nothing was being done to address the mounting problem of juvenile delinquency and crime in general. With the outbreak of the Mau Mau War, there was simply nowhere to put juveniles either convicted or detained without trial for State of Emergency-related offenses. There were officially some 1,600 juveniles in Manyani Camp and at least 2,000 being held throughout the pipeline. It is important to note, however, that the total number of boys detained was, not surprisingly, unrecorded, or at least the records are no longer available.[8] Certainly hundreds if not thousands of these children never saw Wamumu Camp. There was simply not enough room for them, and they instead lived and moved through the other camps with the adult population. Voicing his outrage about the state of youth during this time, Beniah Ohanga, a member of the Kenya Legislative Council, observed:

> No single party within the government wanted to, or could, assume the fiscal or administrative responsibility for these unclaimed children and instead looked to voluntary associations and the missionaries to take care of them. The lack of remand homes (i.e. facilities for juveniles) is nothing short of a scandal, and the judiciary has on many occasions expressed its grave disquiet at the failure of the government to fulfill its statutory obligation to provide remand homes. The situation was hell for the children.[9]

The situation worsened when camps such as Langata, mentioned in Chap. 1, were condemned, and youngsters either were released with nowhere to go or were sent to worse detention camps, such as Manyani. Most colonial officials refused to accept responsibility for the juvenile crisis and instead blamed the Kikuyus and other African parents for not looking after their children in the best traditional forms. As children and young people began to fill transit and detention camps, colonial administrators dealt with young people in contradictory, confusing, and ad hoc ways, alternating between a series of extreme actions, from detention to death to cooptation. However, after 1954 the state began to articulate a clearer and more coherent strategy, and a series of institutions were designed specifically for the management of those youth who were caught up in the State of Emergency; these included youth camps, juvenile reception centers, and youth clubs. This juvenile pipeline was the primary expression of state control over African youth during the State of Emergency period. Through the process, the state sought to rehabilitate young Mau Mau adherents and win over their hearts and minds, halt juvenile migration into Central Province, and seek solutions to the frustrations of the young people who had once sought empowerment by participating in the Mau Mau movement.[10] The juvenile pipeline drew much of its workings from a reservoir of previous youth strategies, experiences, and policies.

It is important to note that the pipeline was the centerpiece of colonial youth control in Kenya during the State of Emergency period. It was a merging of past juvenile policy procedures, colonial government concocted notions of juvenile development and their capacities granted under the State of Emergency Act. The blending of these new apparatuses did not take place directly after the deployment of the Children Welfare Act; instead, piecemeal implementation of some of the salient features of the act took place throughout the 1950s. The development of the pipeline was divided into phases. First, it removed young potential Mau Mau followers from uncontrolled settings such as the Aberdare forests and urban centers and placed them back in reserves or state controlled villages. Secondly, the population of juveniles whom the state considered hardcore Mau Mau activists, a particular subsection of the pipeline who were involved in youth camp migration, vagrancy, and crime, all of which had been aggravated by the State of Emergency regulations, were managed by new and more draconian pipeline procedures.[11]

Despite increased resources and motivation, the state operated in much the same way as it had throughout the past three decades, with minimal rigor, energy, and concrete programs to address the youth problem. Its management of youth, particularly the vagrants and delinquents who were potential Mau Mau activists, during the State of Emergency period was complex and not very effective. It continued to use assorted forms of extreme punishment, threatening suspected Mau Mau youth with armed force, indefinite incarceration, and other forms of inhumane treatment. However, alongside this it also pursued a more rehabilitative course. But even within this framework there were varying extremes. For instance, in the youth camps it sought to reeducate juveniles who had been rounded up during the Mau Mau operations. In reception centers a renewed repatriation scheme was used where the youth were trained in a variety of programs.[12] These courses ranged from literacy courses to labor on government projects. Regardless of all this, the colonial state could not prevent youth migration to Nairobi. Throughout the late 1950s, the state struggled with the increasingly complex situation, and this was clearly evidenced in the juvenile pipeline.

The juvenile pipeline welded together during the State of Emergency period illuminates new perspectives on the state's struggle against and solution to the Mau Mau uprising. By 1953, enough juveniles were being rounded up to warrant official deliberations regarding detention. During this period, Commissioner of Prisons D.G.W. Malone recommended the construction of a separate camp system for juveniles, and his assistant S.H. La Fontaine explored ways in which the young Mau Mau followers could be reintegrated into Kikuyu reserves. While the colonial officials quickly realized that they had no coherent strategy to manage Mau Mau's juvenile ranks, many were firmly in favor of a separate system of institutionalization for Mau Mau youth. Yet the administration was well over a year away from acting on these ideas, and in the meantime the Mau Mau youth found themselves in a variety of institutions.[13] For instance, some were incarcerated in approved schools alongside juvenile delinquents.

As earlier noted, the first responses to the Mau Mau youth problem by the Kenyan colonial government were varied, ad hoc, and contradictory. For instance, in 1954, while the Nairobi Juvenile Court was trying to reunite Mau Mau youth with their families, the probation section of the government was placing them in missions, Nakuru screeners were refusing to transfer them to adult detention, and district commissioners were applying corporal punishment and locking them up alongside adults. Despite a state of confusion in which even young loyalists could be mistaken for Mau Mau followers, most young people rounded up in the first two or three years of the Emergency were placed in transit or detention camps alongside adults. The three facilities to which the bulk of suspected Mau Mau juveniles were transferred were Langata, Kamiti, and Manyani. They were brought in from a variety of areas, but the majority came from Kiambu and Nairobi districts.[14] After Operation Anvil, Manyani added 1200 youths to its preexisting juvenile population. Although hundreds of youths were incarcerated at Kamiti, there was an attempt at Manyani and Langata to return some to their homes. It is evident that the colonial strategy for solving youth problems was confusing, particularly during the phase of resistance and the State of Emergency, and it was not clear to youths themselves why or how they ended up in one or other of the facilities.

It should be noted that youth detention was not the result of a lack of official colonial government policy. The state's first concrete steps toward a more structured, firm, and clear State of Emergency youth policy came in 1953 with the establishment of the Committee on Young Persons and Children, chaired by Humphrey Slade. The committee's mission was to draft measures to protect African youth during the State of Emergency period. Out of Slade's committee came the 1954 Welfare of Children Regulations Act. This provided district commissioners with the authority to round up any African youths whose parents were imprisoned, detained, or "incapacitated" owing to the conflict. Once taken into custody, these youths were placed in approved institutions such as churches, nongovernmental organizations, police offices, and hospitals. While organizations such as the Consolata Mission, Red Cross, and Salvation Army took in hundreds of young people affected by the State of Emergency, few approved institutions were willing to care for more.[15] Many of them, including the Dagoretti Children's Centre, Ujana Park Centre, and Quarry Road Centre, did not have adequate facilities to accommodate hundreds of affected youths. In response, the state was forced to expand the definition of an approved institution to include government-run programs, shifting the burden of care and protection on to itself.

Slade's committee findings were hardly surprising. They reflected commonly held beliefs within the colonial administration regarding young people and how they were supposed to be handled. The notion that modernity and capitalist individualism had broken down traditional African societies, authority, and social norms had entered colonial rhetoric as early as the 1920s. Solutions to the problem were few and far between, but in the 1940s and early 1950s moves were made by the colonial government to provide better alternatives to the problem. By the time of the declaration of the State of Emergency, many colonial officials and settlers believed that the state had a responsibility to protect African children from the supposed primordial psychosis that was afflicting their traditional societies.[16] Providing them with a "civilizing" education was seen as key. For the British, imperialism was not solely about exploitation. Rather, it functioned from their belief that with their superior race, Christian values, and economic knowledge, the British had a duty, a moral obligation, to redeem the "backward heathens" of the world.[17]

In Africa, therefore, the British felt they had an obligation to bring light to the "dark continent" by transforming the so-called natives into progressive citizens, ready to take their place in the modern world. According to them, they were not actually stealing African land or exploiting their labor but were instead self-appointed trustees for the hapless "natives," who had not yet reached a point on the evolutionary scale when they could make independent responsible decisions and use their land for societal progress. The colonial government felt that through "civilizing education" and with proper British guidance and paternalistic love, Africans could be made into progressive men and women. In their estimations, the process could take many decades owing to Africans' inferior academic abilities.[18] To effect the process, colonial officials turned to educators, armed with a citizenship training curriculum, to act as guides who were capable of providing juveniles with the necessary skills and character to navigate the unfamiliar waters of Western modernity and capitalistic needs and processes. It is important to note that the youth civics and citizenship discourse had entered the colonial dialogue in Kenya just prior to the Second World War, and moves were made to create an Empire Youth Movement in the colony as well as to expand the Boy Scouts. It is noteworthy that British officials and settlers looked to inculcate into African youths notions of citizenship, with an emotional attachment to the British Empire. This inculcation was aimed at making African youth fearful of the colonial government and to replace their currently held ideological positions.[19] Its central aim was to make them see the British Empire as the savior of the African continent.

To achieve this, in 1955 the colonial government developed an identifiable strategy that could enable their regulations to operate. The strategy entailed separating young and old detainees and systematizing juvenile detention procedures. Thomas Askwith and the Department of Community Development were given responsibility over the construction of a youth camp system that was designed to cleanse the Mau Mau youth and reintegrate them into society. In July 1955, the government transferred 1200 juveniles out of Manyani, and dozens from Langata and Kamiti, to Wamumu Youth Camp in Embu. Gikubu was among them. It was during this period that he met Geoffrey William Griffin, who would later shape Kenyan youth education and whom Gikubu would work closely with at Manyani, Wamumu, and Starehe Boys Centre and School (SBC) for four decades. Devastated with the effects of the Mau Mau War, Griffin had just resigned from his post as an intelligence officer and was looking for employment. It was during this period that he and Roger Owles applied to the newly created Ministry of Community Development and Rehabilitation and were both taken on as community development officers. By the end of May 1955, Griffin had left for Manyani Detention Camp. Initially, he had expected to be working with adults in village development programs. It was sheer coincidence that on the very morning he reported for duty a major scandal broke out about the incarceration of youth, and reports by eminent clergy, politicians, private citizens, the Red Cross, a former member of Legislative Council Dorothy Hughes, and the British opposition parties on the detention of the juveniles at Manyani had just reached his commissioner in Nairobi. The result was that Griffin and Owles were promptly sent to Manyani, with instructions to check the situation, segregate the juveniles from the adults, and recommend to the colonial government appropriate measures for addressing the matter.

Griffin had no idea what kind of work awaited him when he went to Manyani. He thought that he and Owles were going to form villages and force Kikuyus into them for closer monitoring and training in various developmental programs. Little did he know that a major national undertaking awaited them. Speaking of the prevailing conditions of youth in detention camps, and more generally how these events shaped his future career and involvement in Kenyan youth education, Griffin recalled:

> From Kikuyuland and mostly in barbed wire cages were 20,000 Kikuyus. Among these adults were several youths. And there was screaming and questions were being asked in the British House of Commons and all these were coming to the government. Is this true? Do you have youths in concentration camps? And here I come, a brand new officer, with no duties. So, they said, you get to Manyani. We give you documents to tell the prison authorities to cooperate with you. Check around if you find any children segregate them, and then report to us. This is what brought me in touch with youth education.[20]

It was under these circumstances that Griffin and Owles were summoned and told to go to Manyani Detention Camp to find out the truth of the claims. They were given full authority to investigate the matter and to act accordingly, being required to identify and rehabilitate any young men under the age of twenty. At Manyani, Captain George Gardner was waiting to take charge of their training. These and the events that followed marked the beginning of Griffin and Gikubu's involvement with Kenyan youth education.

Conditions at the Manyani Detention Camp

After the declaration of the State of Emergency and the need to detain numerous Mau Mau rebels, supporters, and sympathizers, there was an increase in the number of convicts at Manyani. Manyani was an enormous site, nearly three miles long by half a mile wide. It was located in a semi-arid and desolate region.[21] The camp had two compounds that were divided by catwalks of barbed wire, which allowed warders to patrol in between the compounds. In the middle, there was a very high tower manned by wardens with machine guns, police dogs, and powerful searchlights to make sure no one escaped. Detainees were housed in low A-frame tin huts with no windows or lights. Each one accommodated 50 prisoners. To avoid trouble, detainees were forced into the huts at three o'clock in the afternoon and were not allowed into the open air until nine o'clock the following day. The camp was staffed by useless drunkards, people who had lost hope in life and were ready to do anything, including killing. The diet was very poor, with no vegetables or fruit. Many detainees suffered from scurvy, kwashiorkor, and marasmus. They did not have adequate clothing, wearing only a pair of yellow short trousers. Describing the conditions, Griffin observed that "the place was a nightmare, very boring, emotional and inhuman. The boys were unresponsive and idle throughout the day. Many detainees were whipped, beaten, sodomized, forced to eat feces and to drink urine by screening teams."[22] Many detainees were sick and mentally ill. Commenting on the horrible conditions from the point of view of a detainee, Gikubu remarked:

> All the detainees had to go through a cattle deep that had medicine. The camp compounds were routinely filled above capacity. Detainees slept on the ground, often one on top of the other. Water supplies were abysmal. Detainees remember drawing drinking water from drainage ditches, swamps, and muddy boreholes. Infectious diseases continued to be ubiquitous in the pipeline. Pulmonary tuberculosis was widely reported. Waterborne infections particularly dysentery, diarrhea, and other epidemic intestinal diseases ran through the camps. So too did vitamin deficiency, with cases of scurvy, pellagra, kwashiorkor, and night blindness. Detainees often slept and ate in the same room where toilet buckets overflowed with urine and faeces. The place was full of bed bugs infested blankets. Detainees slept on cold floors. The rations generally consisted of maize meal, with an occasional piece of meat or vegetable thrown in. The rations were often reduced or completely

taken away as a form of punishment. Many guards beat, tortured, and murdered the detainees without any remorse. The guards were terrible.[23]

Summing up the experiences of former Manyani detainees she interviewed, and backing up the views expressed by Gikubu in my interviews with him, Caroline Elkins writes that "detainees described to me rows of *askaris*, the beatings, the cattle dip, the stripping, a pervasive humiliating atmosphere of strict control and violence, issuance of a single pair of yellow shorts and two blankets, identification metal bands worn on wrists, body searches, struggles over food, and walking shackled."[24] Several medical reports from Manyani at this time indicate that various diseases spread rapidly within the camp, especially typhoid. Commenting on the spread of typhoid, Stoot Henry, the medical adviser to the Labour Department, noted:

> My visit to Manyani was primarily to determine whether typhoid was present and if so to what extent. On the day of my arrival the Medical Officer had performed a post mortem on the body of a man brought in dead from one of the compounds, and it was found that the cause of death had been due to general peritonitis as the result of the perforation of a typhoid ulcer. Several previous cases had been brought in dead from typhoid.[25]

Further, the medical reports also indicate that several visits were made by various medical officers to address the camp's hygiene conditions. The situation was made worse by the lack of regular health officers and of clean water. Additionally, the reports say that the medical authorities were concerned by the number of undiagnosed deaths that were occurring. The figures of dead and sick were very high, but much of this information was concealed by the colonial government. Reporting on the typhoid-related death toll at Manyani in 1954, the *East Africa Standard* noted: "the first case appeared soon after the camp had been opened in April of 1954 and since then there had been 51 deaths from typhoid. By October, typhoid, related cases and deaths had risen to 737."[26] After persistent complaints in medical reports about the detainees' health conditions, including details such as the detainees drank water from the drainage ditches, swamps, and muddy boreholes, the Ministry of Health carried out several measures to address the situation. These included mass inoculations, more medical staff, the flying in of medicine, more isolation compounds, two new hospitals, revaccination, and the appointment of a sister and a health inspector. The

Director of Medical Services and the Minister for Local Government, Health and Housing visited the facility, while the army supplied three laboratory technicians and reorganized laboratory facilities, food handlers were tested, and movement between various compounds was stopped. Additionally, and more prosaically, the camp did not have adequate stationery. It was required to borrow it from other institutions. This occasionally provoked conflict between Manyani and other institutions.[27]

When Griffin and his colleague, Roger Owles, arrived at Manyani, they did not receive a cheerful welcome. The camp officers were reluctant to talk to them, viewing them as government spies who were out to fire them. The promise to remove the youth from the camp did not carry any weight with the officers, and many of them actively opposed the idea. In addition, the detainees viewed Griffin and Owles with suspicion. Despite these early hardships, Griffin and Owles were able to identify 2,000 youths of 17 years or younger, whom they placed in separate compounds before appointing several youth leaders to help run these new compounds. Gikubu was among them. He was appointed the head of all the youths at Manyani, his team being tasked with building discipline among the youths. Once this had been established, Gikubu was requested to assist in designing and supervising the teaching of various literacy skills and trades, such as carpentry, masonry, and agriculture. Griffin and Gikubu's team succeeded in creating an interest among the youths in learning various trades. These early and basic trial and error educational experiments laid the foundation for their later involvement in Kenyan youth education. Speaking of the effect of Manyani on this, Gikubu noted: "although the conditions at the camp were tough, the place made me discover my love for youth education. Although the skills we taught the youth were basic, I discovered various ways of leading, teaching and interacting with them."[28] The process gave Gikubu hope, courage, confidence, and recognition of his abilities in youth education and their potential in societal development.

It is vital to note that despite the significant role Gikubu and other leaders played in providing discipline and some trade skills for the youth at Manyani, an examination of the colonial literature demonstrates that many of the colonial officers viewed them as cooperators, and there was some discussion that they should be employed at Manyani in service to the colonial government. A letter from the Ministry of Defence to the Secretary for Community Development on the subject dated August 8, 1956 attests to this. It reads:

The Community Development Officer at Manyani states that he wishes to retain at Manyani some of his pupil-teachers. Being co-operators, these detainees would normally be moved out as soon as possible. At present Special Branch are retaining and employing at Manyani a number of detainees and it would be possible to arrange the retention of some pupil teachers on the same basis. If you agree, and can provide funds to pay these detainees, I suggest that the Community Development Officer be asked to arrange this directly with the commandant. This Ministry will have no objection.[29]

A critical examination of the academic activities that were undertaken by Gikubu during this period reveal simple, modest, unstructured, and basic educational activities. Although most of the educational activities functioned under colonial rehabilitation policies, there is clear evidence of ingenuity and brilliance, especially in the wide variety of trades that were offered despite the lack of essential learning tools. Through the Manyani rehabilitation program, Gikubu learnt a lot about youth psychology, leadership, academic abilities, and their role in school administration. With inadequate resources and little assistance, Griffin, his colleagues, and the student leaders under the stewardship of Gikubu had to rely on their own initiatives and imaginations to fashion a wide range of educational activities. It was a demanding undertaking. These early experiences were further expanded at Wamumu, when Gikubu and other youths were relocated there at the end of June 1955.

It was the initial success of these simple educational ventures that convinced Griffin and his colleagues that they should ask the government to relocate the youth to a new site, where they could be offered more educational training. As far as they were concerned, they had accomplished their mission at Manyani. In response to Griffin's request, the government built a brand new camp at Wamumu. The process of relocation was difficult, especially from the standpoint of the officers at Manyani who were not ready to back Griffin and his colleague. When the Special Branch police who dealt with state security learned of Griffin's plans to relocate youth to Wamumu they opposed the idea. Several arguments ensued, but in the end Griffin and Owles were permitted to go ahead with their plans for a rehabilitation center.

It is important to note that when youths were initially confined at Manyani, Gikubu was 16 years old. It was after they had been at Manyani for a while that they began to receive rehabilitation officers. Over time detainees began to surrender, while others confessed their participation in the Mau Mau movement. At the end of the process, 2,000 youths were selected and relocated to Wamumu. It is essential to note that this relocation was not immediate: the detainees were told they would be relocated, but nothing happened. In addition, there were several false rumors pertaining to the relocation and other detention matters, such as external help coming from the United Nations and the British Labour Party, the defeat of the colonial government, and the nearing of independence. The detainees called this secret circulation of news the *Manyani Times*, *By Way of the Wire*, the *Kimongo Times*, or the *Nyandarua Times*. It was all propaganda or deliberately false rumors, fabricated by detainees to encourage other inmates and to compel them to resist any temptation to confess or to cooperate with camp authorities.[30] These false rumors gave detainees hope that one day they would be released. It took two more years before Gikubu and other detainees were relocated to Wamumu. Recalling this, Gikubu remarked:

> One day, the time arrived for us to leave. We were placed in a train. We were each given two loaves of bread, two blankets and we took the Nanyuki route, passed through Sagana. At Sagana we were removed from the train, counted and then packed into other lorries and taken to Wamumu. The journey took more than twelve hours. We had mixed emotions when we arrived at Wamumu. We did not know what the future held for us.[31]

This chapter underscores the early involvement of Gikubu in Kenyan youth education during his incarceration at Manyani Detention Camp. Despite the many challenges that he and other detainees experienced there, the place helped him discover his gifts for youth education. Through his leadership and trade work with the detained youths, he gained several educational and administrative skills. His role as an effective youth leader contributed enormously to the youths' early transfer to Wamumu in order to be given more educational opportunities. It was these minimal educational skills and administrative lessons that Gikubu tried to improve on at Wamumu and Othaya Approved School. To him, Manyani was his "University of Hard Knocks." It was the "University of Life," which allowed him to discover his talents in educational leadership and youth education in general. Manyani Detention Camp paved the way for his greater engagement in Kenyan youth education.

NOTES

1. Caroline Elkins, *Imperial Reckoning: The Untold Story of Britain's Gulag in Kenya* (New York: Henry Holt and Company, 2005), 168.
2. Ibid., 103.
3. Ibid., 105.
4. Atieno Odhiambo and John Lonsdale, *Mau Mau and Nationhood: Arms, Authority and Narration* (Athens: Ohio University Press, 2003), 106.
5. Elkins, *Imperial Reckoning: The Untold Story of Britain's Gulag in Kenya*, 108.
6. Ibid.
7. Paul Ocobock, "Joy Rides for Juveniles: Vagrant Youth and Colonial Control in Nairobi, Kenya, 1901–1952," *Social History*, 31.1(2006): 39–59.
8. Tabitha, Kanogo, *Squatters and the Roots of Mau Mau* (London: James Currey, 1987), 69.
9. Ibid., 290.
10. Ocobock, "Joy Rides for Juveniles: Vagrant Youth and Colonial Control in Nairobi, Kenya, 1901–1952".
11. Ibid.
12. Peter Ojiambo, *Teaching Beyond Teaching: Geoffrey William Griffin and Starehe Boys Centre and School*. Saarbrucken, Germany: VDM Verlag, 2008.
13. Ibid.
14. Kennedy Hongo and Jesse Mugambi, *Starehe Boys Centre: School and Institute. The First Forty Years 1959–1999* (Nairobi: Acton Publishers, 2003).
15. Benjamin Kipkorir, *Biographical Essays on Imperialism and Colonialism in Colonial Kenya* (Nairobi: Kenya Literature Bureau, 1980).
16. Ocobock, "Joy Rides for Juveniles: Vagrant Youth and Colonial Control in Nairobi, Kenya, 1901–1952".
17. Elkins, *Imperial Reckoning: The Untold Story of Britain's Gulag in Kenya*, 6.
18. Kennedy Hongo and Jesse Mugambi, *Starehe Boys Centre: School and Institute. The First Forty Years 1959–1999*.
19. Ibid.
20. Television Interview, Geoffrey Griffin, October, 2000.
21. Kipkorir, *Biographical Essays on Imperialism and Colonialism in Colonial Kenya*.
22. Yusuf King'ala, *The Autobiography of Geoffrey William Griffin: Kenya's Champion Beggar* (Nairobi: Falcon Crest, 2005), 145.
23. Interview, Joseph Gikubu, August 9, 2012.
24. Ibid., 374.
25. Medical Report KNA/43/10B/57 by Stoot Henry, the medical adviser to the Labour Department on his visit to Manyani concerning the rampant spread of diseases at the camp, especially typhoid.

26. East African Standard Newspaper Report KNA/33/333/vol.11/77A on the death tolls at Manyani in 1954 that were typhoid related.
27. A memo KNA/ADM/61/47 from the Prisons Department dated August 9, 1957, complaining about lack of adequate stationery at Manyani and the occasional conflicts that arose between Manyani and other institutions in its attempts to address the situation.
28. Interview, Joseph Gikubu, August 11, 2013.
29. A letter KNA/EMER.45/13/1/14A-196 from the Ministry of Defence to the Secretary for Community Development on August 8, 1956 on the need to employ Gikubu and other student leaders at Manyani for their cooperation in the colonial rehabilitation efforts.
30. Kanogo, *Squatters and the Roots of Mau Mau*.
31. Interview, Joseph Gikubu, August 11, 2012.

CHAPTER 3

A Place of Hope: Wamumu Rehabilitation Camp ("Eton of Africa")

The greater involvement of Gikubu in Kenyan youth education can be traced to Wamumu Rehabilitation Camp. Wamumu, or the "Eton of Africa" as it was commonly known, was the first of the several youth camps built by the Ministry of Community Development in Central Province during the State of Emergency. It was the largest of all the rehabilitation camps and performed most of the rehabilitative work on young Mau Mau suspects. The true title of Wamumu and its true mission was often debated among colonial officials. It is referenced in various colonial literature as a rehabilitation camp, an approved school, a youth camp, or a works camp. There was correspondence between Captain George Gardner, the officer in charge of Wamumu, and Thomas Askwith, the Commissioner for Community Development and Rehabilitation, on the matter, as illustrated in the following communication from Gardner:

> On receipt of the letter MCD/18/1/424 of the 17th September 1955, from the Assistant Secretary for Community Development, we styled this institution as *Wamumu Camp*. This title appeared to find general favor as being apt, and descriptive of the actual function of Wamumu. The District Commissioner has pointed out, however that the detainees here as opposed to the approved school boys can only be held in a "*Works Camp*" and he has requested me to obtain Ministerial approval for the use of the title "*Youth Camp*".[1]

In his response, Askwith consented to The Wamumu Juveniles Rehabilitation Camp and Approved School as the official titles, as opposed to its previous name: Wamumu Works Camp. The lack of a clear title for Wamumu confirms the argument in Chap. 2 with regard to the colonial government's lack of clear policies on youth vagrancy and the fact that one institution could perform multiple functions, as was the case with Wamumu. It also demonstrates the colonial hidden agenda that undergirded the purpose and programs that were carried out at Wamumu. In its early years it functioned as a detention facility, later becoming a rehabilitation camp and an approved school.

Wamumu was gazetted in 1955. Little did the colonial officials know that this small and makeshift detention facility for suspected Mau Mau youth would outlive them and go on to perform much of their rehabilitative work. According to the KNA DC/EMB/2/1/1 report by E.P.B. Derrick, the District Commissioner of Embu, which is dated March 1959, a juvenile confined at Wamumu was required to fit one of the following criteria: no parent or guardian, abandoned by parents or guardian, detained in circumstances related to the State of Emergency, lacking a home or with a poor home that could not support him, or having a home that was so bad the child had to be taken away from it. Originally, the camp housed youths who had been detained at Manyani, nearly all of whom had been picked up by Operation Anvil. According to the Annual Report of the Department of Community Development and Rehabilitation, 1956, administrators within the Ministry quickly discovered that the camp held rehabilitative potential and was ideal for youth activities.

Askwith believed that the experience gained at Wamumu would be of great importance, because it had become clear over the years that the most intractable problem in Kenya was the training of adolescents in active citizenship, patriotism to the colonial government, and community engagement. By December 1956, the camp was receiving several juveniles. An examination of communications from the Commissioner of Prisons to the Secretary for Community Development and Rehabilitation during this period show that juveniles were still being held in various detention camps within the country, and there were orders to the officers in charge of them to examine and transfer them to Wamumu, in consultation with the rehabilitation staff from the Ministry of Community Development and Rehabilitation. Although Wamumu was only meant to accommodate juveniles who were under 18 years, records indicate that there were several over-age youths held there. There were numerous requests throughout 1957 from the Secretary of Defence to the Wamumu management for their possible removal and relocation to other camps or their placement in the adult pipeline.

Gikubu's increasing involvement in Kenyan youth education can be traced to Wamumu. It was here that his leadership prowess was sharpened and many of the educational experiments that had begun at Manyani were put to test. As Griffin was only 20 years of age and Roger Owles slightly older, Askwith felt they were too young to be left on their own to run Wamumu. Captain George Gardner was thus seconded from the Royal Engineers to take charge of the camp (Fig. 3.1). Gardner was a 55-year-old engineer with considerable experience in social welfare work who had been in the British Army during the Second World War. Griffin and Owles were appointed junior officers to him, both having just completed their short service with Kenyan African Rifles. The fourth officer at Wamumu was

Fig. 3.1 Captain George Gardner, officer in-charge of Wamumu (Photo by author from Starehe School archives)

George Dennis, an expert in carpentry who had initially worked at Athi River Works Camp. Griffin was in charge of administration while Owles and Dennis supervised the daily projects. Remembering Wamumu's leadership, Gikubu said: "it was great leadership, very meticulous, organized, understanding, and cooperative in all its work. As a youth leader, I enjoyed working with them."[2]

At Wamumu, the rehabilitation scheme developed by Askwith and discussed in Chap. 2 was put to work. According to the Rehabilitation Progress Report of 1955, by the end of September 1955, approximately 1,800 juveniles between the ages of 16 and 20 were being housed there and were turning out 1,000 bricks a day to construct various facilities that the camp required to make it livable in and operational. The camp was very much a detention camp in the early years. Brand new, very much like Manyani, it was surrounded by barbed wire and had armed warders and A-frame huts. Given the nature of its work, Wamumu was run independently of other camps in Embu District. Continuity among the staff was seen as important in view of its long-term nature. At the same time cooperation and coordination with other rehabilitation works in Embu District were vital. The camp was under the direction of the Ministry of Community Development. Youths were only admitted if they were committed by a court under the provisions of the Juvenile Ordinance of 1934 and after confirmation had been given by the Chief Inspector of Approved Schools that accommodation was available within the school's financial provisions, which limited the number of youths who could be accommodated to 250. All rules made under the Juveniles Ordinance of 1934 pertaining to diet, discipline, and the management of approved schools applied to Wamumu. There was a great emphasis on discipline, but instruction was also given in various trades such as agriculture, carpentry, and masonry. The site of the camp on Mwea plains was well chosen. It was in a healthy district with plenty of agricultural land around it, and it was hoped that with time it would be self-supporting in all its operations. The aim of the Wamumu rehabilitation program was to rehabilitate all the young detainees at Manyani and later all those in other camps irrespective of their previous past—whether they had killed, taken the Mau Mau oath, or were just Mau Mau followers or sympathizers (Figs. 3.2, 3.3, and 3.4).

Getting youths to develop trust in Griffin and his colleagues at Wamumu was a gradual process. At first they were highly suspicious of the intentions of the camp officers. They kept wondering why they had been taken to Wamumu, some even thinking that they were going to be killed. It took

Fig. 3.2 Wamumu Rehabilitation Camp entrance gate (Photo by author from Starehe School archives)

Fig. 3.3 Youths at Wamumu ready to participate in daily activities (Photo by author from Starehe School archives)

Fig. 3.4 Youths participating in physical education at Wamumu (Photo by author from Starehe School archives)

time for them to develop their trust in camp officers, despite the constant promise to them that they could be released to their families if they reformed.

The first two months at Wamumu were difficult for youths and the staff alike. From early in the morning to late in the evening, the youths were kept busy by digging ditches, making roads, and building classrooms and workshops. Commenting on these early hardships, Griffin remarked:

> We had a hard time at first because the boys when they first arrived were filled with apathy, they wouldn't look at you and many of them wouldn't even talk to you. They just sat stubborn. We knew that somewhere, within them there were leaders among them who were holding them, whom they feared and were not letting anybody co-operate even if it meant getting on the way of freedom. And until we could find out who these people were and get rid of them, our hands were tied. We couldn't make much progress.[3]

Griffin and his colleagues had to fight from the onset to remove the hardcore youths who were unruly and had made several attempts to escape from the camp. Gardner, Griffin, and other officers used various means to exile them. A purge was carried out, and several of those involved in the escape were expelled and sent to tougher prisons. Commenting on this security approach, in his communication to the Commissioner for Community Development and Rehabilitation that detailed the various heinous activities of 32 hardcore youths at Wamumu in the early days, Gardner noted:

> There are in this camp about thirty-two detainees who are hardcore, irreconcilable, Mau Mau. Most of these are at the top of the age-group we cater for. They were reported as having tried to indoctrinate other boys with Mau Mau, they had formed a kind of "escape syndicate", they had been manufacturing illicit knives, obtaining money, and documents. There are about forty more boys who are under suspicion for similar activities, but we consider that we have the ring leaders in the first thirty-two. A firm example is most necessary, and I recommend that they be sent to an exile camp forthwith.[4]

The removal of these youths from the camp cooled the atmosphere at Wamumu. Slowly the youths begun to confess their wrongdoings and to actively participate in various rehabilitation activities. The rehabilitation program was a staggering success. The entries, searchlights, and watchtowers that were placed in the compound disappeared within the first year, while the youths built classrooms and churches, as well as forming sport teams and a scout troop. Employers spoke enthusiastically of their ex-Wamumu recruits, and the attorney general issued a blank pardon for all former crimes to every youth who passed successfully through the camp. According to Roger Martin, "the boys sang all day in their own tongue as they worked and played. Their music transformed the wilderness and gladdened the hearts of the young officers who had brought the barren camp to life."[5] Gikubu noted that, owing to its rapid success, the youths became joyful and hopeful about what Wamumu had done for them and what it was capable of doing for them in the future, to the extent that they developed many false rumors popularly nicknamed the *Wamumu Times*, mentioned in Chap. 2. For instance, there were rumors that they would be provided with reading books, with teachers, would receive more education, or would soon be released and be given employment.

The success of Wamumu within a relatively short period was confounding. Explaining this, Griffin noted:

> Within a year, the double-banked barbed wire that surrounded the camp came down. When we began, there were about 200 armed guards to make sure that the boys did not run away. These were reduced to 40, who were needed for

outside guarding to make sure that Mau Mau fighters did not interfere with our work. We used a gradual process in giving the boys freedom. Youth leaders like Gikubu were vital to Wamumu's success. Without Gikubu's leadership we would not have managed to achieve our mission.[6]

Within a year, youngsters who had been tough and insolent were transformed into obedient, trusted, and useful citizens ready to go and develop their communities. The great achievement of the rehabilitation program inspired Governor Baring, who visited the camp in 1956 during his tour under the State of Emergency, to grant the Wamumu youths amnesty. He declared: "any boy, going through Wamumu and through your hands and being released by you because you are satisfied with him, I give a free pardon of any crime he has committed including murder."[7] After a year, rehabilitated youths were repatriated to their home areas and given jobs by the government. In addition, they were exempted from a ban which prevented members of Kikuyu, Embu, and Meru from travelling in Kenya or getting jobs.

Wamumu's success allowed the Special Branch officers to leave the camp earlier than planned. It became essential that they should leave because Griffin, his colleagues, and the student leaders expressed their intention to run a school and not a detention camp. From the beginning, Griffin and his colleagues proposed to transform Wamumu from a jail to a school, even though the juveniles included at least 60 youths who had taken human life and hundreds more with tough records. This purpose was clearly expressed in Gardner's words to the youths in his first inaugural speech to them:

> Gentlemen, I hope you enjoyed your long journey from Manyani, the place I know you all hate. I'd like you to know that this is not a prison. Here you will obey, keep yourselves clean, tell no lies, and work hard. If you co-operate, you will learn many things which shall help you, your families and your country in future.[8]

The Wamumu staff believed that young Mau Mau suspects had to be managed separately as well as differently from their adult counterparts. They argued that their crimes had been committed under the stimulus of a general ethnic movement, with the youth imitating their elders in a condition of genuine, albeit misguided, enthusiasm. The degree of guilt could not be considered as equivalent to that incurred when such crimes were committed for personal reasons. It is because of this recognition, that from the beginning Gardner's team and the student leaders strived to put in place educational programs at Wamumu that could benefit youth. By December 1955, Wamumu began functioning more like a school. To achieve this, the camp required a facelift. With voluntary labor from the youths in their spare time, trees and hedges were planted. Locker rooms, tables, and seats were built from bricks in the dormitories, which together with the recreation rooms and other buildings made Wamumu a much more habitable place. As the New Year began, the inmates began to build an institution for their rehabilitation rather than their detention.

It was at Wamumu that Gikubu's leadership skills were exhibited and enhanced. He was appointed the school captain and was placed in charge of school discipline and trade classes. Recalling his leadership qualities, Griffin noted:

> Gikubu was a natural leader. He was a man of courage and conviction. His leadership talent made our administrative work easier. He enabled us to excel in all the activities we undertook. Without his lead, our work would have failed totally. He was so efficient that we regarded him more as a colleague than a detainee.[9]

From the moment when the youths were transferred to Wamumu, Gikubu was involved in their transformation. As a student leader, he was tasked with ensuring that the youths were disciplined and that any hardcore criminals were identified and removed from the camp. Planning daily activities was his responsibility. He ensured that the compound was clean and that the youths were assigned various duties. In the early days, since the work was seemingly never-ending, he ensured that the youths continued to be motivated and were continually engaged in various activities such as cleaning the compound, making fences, and constructing classrooms. When trade classes began, after the camp had been built, Gikubu was instrumental in advising youths which courses to take and assisted with the teaching before appropriate instructors were hired. In addition to these duties, Gikubu also took the lead in establishing several academic and cocurricular programs, which became the hallmark of Wamumu: Baraza (student parliament), student freedom, agriculture, sporting activities, academic programs, scouting, spiritual activities, boarding houses, community service, old boys' society and reunions, school traditions, and discipline. Each of these will be briefly discussed.

Barazas were very useful in terms of camp management. Youths were encouraged to speak openly about their past experiences in a free and relaxed atmosphere. This helped the camp run smoothly, and several problems were detected fast and promptly addressed. Barazas also cultivated trust between the students and the camp administrators. Sessions were led by Gikubu every Friday evening, lasting for two hours.

Granting students freedom was key to the success of Wamumu. Gikubu was instrumental in ensuring that youths who confessed their mistakes and reformed were granted freedom gradually. This enabled mutual trust to develop. As a sign of gratitude for being granted freedom, the youths reciprocated by conducting themselves well and assisting in various Wamumu programs. They were no longer locked up in their dormitories at night; they had the freedom to do whatever they liked. In addition, visits of parents and relatives were always encouraged, and a special building was constructed where youths could be met in private. The number of visits increased monthly throughout the year.

For those youths who had interest in land, Gikubu worked closely with the administration to start an agricultural program. This was irrigated by the camp's waste water. When not learning in classrooms, the youths worked in a five-acre school farm to make the camp self-sustaining. They grew various crops, and in later periods fresh food that the school had grown elicited the admiration of many visitors. With access to a herd of cattle, the youths were taught animal husbandry courses. A section was also opened for a dairy, and this was later extended to pigs and chickens.

Gikubu loved sports. He was heavily involved in this area and worked tirelessly to ensure that all youths were able to participate in a variety of sports. From the outset he ensured that they created playing fields, and within a year they had at least 14 full-size soccer playing fields complete with an athletic track and a boxing ring. There were interhouse football competitions each month, and strong interhouse rivalry in various sports. In addition, the youths competed in adult district leagues, athletic meetings, boxing, football, volleyball, basketball, tug of war, and physical training. Sporting competitions were also held between Wamumu and other institutions, such as Kigari Teachers College, Kabete Approved School, and Kangaru Government African School. In all competitions Wamumu performed well, winning several awards. Wamumu youths were also frequently invited to give gymnastic displays at the Royal Shows in Embu, Nairobi, and other parts of the country. They also conducted special parades during yearly Empire Day celebrations. Their morale and discipline in all these activities were high and admirable. Sporting activities under the leadership of Gikubu "made Wamumu's stature strong and a good showcase within the colonial rehabilitation programs. They brought Wamumu's rehabilitation work to the larger Kenyan public."[10]

Academic programs were part of the earliest activities. In the early days, Gikubu ensured that the youths were engaged in setting up the required infrastructure, such as constructing classrooms. In all, the camp had 20 open-sided classrooms. It fulfilled a longstanding need within the colony, and the visit of Governor Baring on December 20, 1955, was considered the final recognition and approval of Wamumu's academic programs. In addition, in January 1956 the classroom block and workshops opened. Classes flourished, demonstrating high standards of teaching. There were workshops for training in various trades such as carpentry, blacksmithing, shoemaking, tailoring, painting, signwriting, motor mechanics, and mechanical engineering. Youths were also trained in Kiswahili, English, elementary literacy, and arithmetic. A system where senior youths spent six weeks in the classroom and three weeks in the trade shop of their choice was also developed and enhanced. Expansion of academic programs "marked the fulfillment of one of the earliest promises made to the in-mates by Gardner that facilities for their education would be provided and they would receive an education that would provide them essential life skills."[11] Towards the latter end of 1956, Wamumu was allowed to register youths for examinations, with the hope that they would gain admission into the new Railway Training School, where they undertake a high-quality five-year apprenticeship program. The examinations consisted of academic papers, character-based tests, rigorous physical training, and manual tasks. Almost all youths from Wamumu passed these entry examinations, gaining 20 places, with 40 schools taking part. Demonstrating the importance that Gardner, his team, and student leaders attached to providing quality trades for the youths, there were constant requests from Gardner to the Secretary for Community Development asking for more instructors to assist Gikubu and the administrators.

Scouting was one of the earliest activities that was introduced by Gikubu to Wamumu. Having been a scout himself in primary school, he loved adventure and wanted the Wamumu youths to experience it too. Many of them gained the coveted First Class Badge, which was almost unknown among African troops at the time. Several of the senior scouts were capable of going on to the highest rank in scouting in the colony—Queen's Scout—which would have earned them the Royal Certificate, but they invariably qualified for release before this could come to pass owing to the tremendous reformation that was taking place at Wamumu. Five weeks' camping was always conducted during the months of August and September, and many youths qualified for various outdoor badges. Wamumu scout troops provided several guards of honor for important visitors who visited the camp. In addition, they assisted at various national events.

Gikubu ensured that the youths participated in various religious activities every week. They built their own church with a sitting capacity of 500 people in five weeks, at a cost of 152,000 Kenya shillings that was donated by the Roman Catholic Bishop of Nyeri, the Rt. Rev. Charles Cavallera. It was a grass-thatched building made from mud and wattle walls. There were plans to erect a second church for the Protestant congregation by early 1957. Further, there were also Christian teachings offered by various members of the Wamumu staff, visiting padres, and the Navigator Organization. Various religious films were shown every month by the Christian Council of Kenya. Commenting on the religious aspects of the camp and the instruction and training that was provided for the youth, Hongo and Mugambi observe that "during the year over 490 youths were baptized into the Protestant faith and several moving cleansing ceremonies were held for the boys who wanted church's aid in spiritual decontamination from Mau Mau. Over 300 further youths were received into the Roman Catholic fold."[12]

To facilitate the easy management of the youths, Gikubu helped the administration to establish various boarding houses. The 1,200 youths at Wamumu were divided into five boarding houses, namely, Boyes, Delamere, Grogan, Lugard, and Junior. Each of these was managed by an African housemaster, an assistant, a captain, and a house prefect. Each boarding house had an office, a recreation room, and a kitchen. It was here that Gikubu played a leading role as the head captain of the student body. He supervised all the youths within the camp and oversaw the smooth running of the boarding houses. He ensured there were high levels of discipline, that the youths were engaged in the running of their school, and that they were doing well in academic and non-academic activities. He conducted weekly meetings with all the boarding houses to address any emerging challenges and to ensure that they were effectively managed.

Community service was one of the key activities that Gikubu was heavily involved in. This was reflected in Wamumu's flag. At its center it had the motto of "Truth and Loyalty in a wheel of progress," combined with a cross of religion. There were also tools representing work, the torch of learning, and the lion of Kenya. The hoisting of this flag gratified Gardner, his colleagues, and the youths. It signified the future service of the reformed youths of Wamumu to Kenyan society. To facilitate their engagement in community service work, Gikubu was tasked with linking students to various community projects and supervising their work. Almost every weekend they were actively involved in various activities.

Gikubu assisted the youths in forming an old boys' society and conducting their reunions. Depending on his work schedule, he ensured he attended these meetings. Commenting on these meetings, Gardner reported to the Principal Probation Officer on June 6, 1956, that:

> At one stage there were over five hundred old and new students of Wamumu. It was a really amazing sight, and I am happy to be able to report that every boy conducted himself in a "Wamumu style." Both the new and old boys of Wamumu mingled freely. It was a testimony to the quality of our programs. I was proud to have been part of it.[13]

Under Gikubu's leadership numerous school traditions also evolved within the first year, aimed at fostering Wamumu's unique character. For instance, "boys, who were due for release, on the evening preceding their departure, stood on the small dais near the flagpole during the ceremony of retreat."[14] Reveille was played each morning at six o'clock and retreat at six in the evening, at which all youths had to be at attention. And on Empire Day a special parade and lecture were held, at which all youths learned the "glorious history and inheritance of the British Empire."[15] The significance of these ceremonies was carefully explained by Gikubu to all the new youths.

Discipline was one of the earliest tasks that Gikubu embarked on after the youths arrived. This was the hallmark of Wamumu's rehabilitative work and it was why the camp was known and respected throughout the colony. Gikubu ensured that the youths were disciplined appropriately and that any misbehavior was promptly addressed. Camp officials marveled at the discipline throughout Wamumu's existence. Out of the 6,000 articles of clothing issued to the youths, only three were damaged. The youths also demonstrated discipline amongst themselves: for example, escapees were hunted down by their fellow youths and returned. According to the annual report of the Ministry of Community Development in 1958, even after their release ex-Wamumu inmates were praised for their discipline and dedication to work at the various places they worked.

In order to ease their workload, Gardner and his colleagues decided to incorporate youths who had leadership skills into the main administrative structure. Kennedy Hongo and Jesse Mugambi observe that "it was impossible for a tiny handful of European Officers to supervise the intimate daily discipline of a camp containing 1,800 youths, and it was necessary to foster a reliable prefect system."[16] The prefects were reliable, capable, and worthy of the confidence that was entrusted to them. Because of the good working relationships that were forged at Wamumu, many of these prefects later became cornerstones in the building of Starehe Boys Centre and School (SBC). Key among them were Geoffrey Gatama Geturo, who was in charge of the main office, and Gikubu, who was the head youth and a first-class prefect in charge of the short-term corrective courses for hardcore vagrants. Both were superb prefects at Wamumu. Affirming this, Griffin noted: "Gikubu and Geturo and were efficient leaders in their handling of difficult youths. They were natural leaders and whatever I couldn't break through they did."[17] It was these outstanding leadership qualities that in later years Griffin tapped into when he begun Starehe and Kariokor youth clubs and later SBC. Gardner credits much of Wamumu's success to his officers and to Gikubu's leadership prowess as a prefect. He noted:

> I must pay tribute to the wonderful support I have received from all members of the staff, particularly Dennis, Griffin, Owles, and the youth leaders, especially, Joseph Gikubu. Gikubu's loyalty, cooperation, and devotion to duty has been a great inspiration to all the youths and everyone in the camp. He has created a strong team spirit among students that has been largely responsible for the wonderful atmosphere that exists throughout the camp. The youths progress in all areas would not have been possible without his lead.[18]

It can be argued that Wamumu was the testing ground that affirmed Gikubu's belief in youth education. It convinced him of the role of youths in societal development if they were given a rich education. Although many of the educational activities that were offered at Wamumu were improvised by Gardner, his colleagues, and Gikubu's youth team, in order to adequately comprehend them it is imperative to understand the colonial rehabilitative policies and mentalities under which they functioned, which were discussed in Chap. 2. The business at Wamumu was not simply about discipline and order; rather, its goals were far loftier: the treatment of the "Mau Mau disease." Such therapy required two procedures: the removal of Mau Mau ideology and its replacement with ideas of citizenship and the development of practical, employable skills which would allow inmates to participate in the development of the colony. Rehabilitation policy was threefold. First, was the spiritual decontamination of the Mau Mau oath from the youths' minds. To accomplish this, Louis Leakey's prescription of Christian confession was implemented. Wamumu officials demanded full disclosure. Part of the youths' religious conversion involved "cleansing" ceremonies performed on them. At the camp, the Christian influence permeated every activity and program. State-sponsored exorcisms were not the only tools employed by camp officials. Football, boxing, masculine activities, and most of the cocurricular activities at the camp were also an integral part of Wamumu's construction of loyal colonial citizens.[19]

The second component of rehabilitation was the forging of colonial citizens through reeducation and character training programs. To accomplish this, the camp was run on lines almost identical to the British military service and public school system. School traditions became an integral part of discipline and the colonial state strived to bond with the African community. Paul Ocobock notes that:

> Wamumu inmates had to connect in more intimate and material ways with the colonial state. In his monthly reports, Gardner always noted the number of circumcisions the camp medical dresser would perform on the youths, sometimes a dozen or more each month. Not only was the state presenting itself as a guardian, and a family with a vast imperial kinship network, but also the social guarantor of the transition into adulthood.[20]

But for many Kikuyu youths at Wamumu, young adulthood meant little without land and freedom. In June 1956, an agricultural officer was called to the camp because the inmates were showing a considerable interest in the land consolidations and agricultural activities that were taking place in Kikuyu reserves and in other parts of Central Province. Thus, the rehabilitation program at Wamumu took on a third characteristic: transforming the youths through education and technical training into a literate, skilled laboring class employable in colonial industries and administration.[21] The camp provided senior youths with six weeks of training and three weeks of in-shop experience with carpenters, blacksmiths, and fitters. It also provided two fields for agriculture and livestock herding. Prior to an inmate's release, the Department of Community Development made arrangements for job placement. In 1956, according to the Annual Wamumu reports, 79 juveniles trained in masonry, carpentry, blacksmithing, and agriculture were sent to the Rift Valley Province to fill various vacancies and another 126 boys were sent to Nairobi. The Kenya Sisal Growers Association took about 200 Wamumu youths in 1957 to work at their various plantations. Several youths were also given employment in the police force and civil service, quite possibly becoming part of the colony's counterinsurgency movement and collaborators in preventing any anticipated uprising against the colonial government.[22]

Debates on Wamumu Programs

An in-depth examination of Wamumu's educational programs demonstrates that they were a success. The intention was to equip the youths physically, academically, and mentally with skills that upon their return to their villages they would utilize to rebuild their broken lives and that of their societies. It was clear throughout their stay that the youths greatly changed in their outlook to life in general. Work was no longer hated but, rather, was seen as a source of pride. When there was work to be done, Owles announced it over the camps trumpet. He would ask for five volunteers but would get 50. Cheerful smiles, laughter, and courteous greetings supplanted the youths' earlier hostility and insolence. More youths were taken to their homes as and when opportunities rose both as propaganda and as a sign of the success of their training. Colonial officials were convinced of the success of Wamumu. Within a year, "every aspect of the camp was changed. Mau Mau was not only discarded, it was almost forgotten."[23] The programs and discipline became well known throughout the colony, and many young detainees in several camps strived to be transferred to Wamumu. Once finished with their training, the inmates were released back to their districts or given employment in various parts of the country. Job opportunities in Nairobi took a considerable number of the Wamumu youths, given that the expulsion of tens of thousands of Kikuyus, Embus, and Merus from the city created a severe labor shortage. The 1956 annual report lauds the transformation of several Mau Mau youths who had been trained at Wamumu. Once free from the camp, the influence of rehabilitation did not wane, at least in the minds of those in the colonial administration. When the police investigated crimes in which Wamumu youths were suspect, the juveniles needed only to show their leaving certificates and they were absolved of any accusation.

Commenting on their overall joy at the success of the program, Griffin opined that "the transformation we made in the lives of the youths was heartwarming. Less than a year back the youth were on their journeys end in a ghastly detention as condemned criminals. But now, they were alive, vibrant and on their total freedom."[24] In July 1956, the first releases were made of the 20 outstanding youths, whose detention orders were suspended so that they could be taken on as paid staff by Wamumu. With time, more and more releases followed, providing proof of the efficacy of the programs. Wherever the Wamumu youths went for employment, they won praise. In many cases, employers asked for more of them and were ready to create vacancies to absorb them. After an initial period of suspicion, the Wamumu administration discovered that the youths not only kept out of trouble after their release but also set an example of good behavior to others in their respective employments and communities. The district commissioners of Nairobi, Thika, and Kiambu districts, which took the bulk of the early releases, expressed their utmost satisfaction with the work of ex-Wamumu youths.

The success of Wamumu was also evidenced in the several honors it received in cocurricular activities. For instance, in 1957 Wamumu was among the institutions that were honored by the Queen. In that year, among the seven Kenya scouts who were honored and awarded Queen's Scout Badges four of them were from Wamumu. Saluting Wamumu for its great excellence in scouting and student leadership partnership, a *Weekly Digest Magazine* editorial in 1957 noted:

> The fact that four of the new recipients are from the Wamumu School says much for the outstanding spirit being engendered in this African "Boys town" by the officer in-charge, Captain George Gardner and his staff. Two of these youths are former detainees and his staff that achieved a first-class record in the school, have now become members of the school staff and are passing on to others what they have learned. The third, a detainee is the school captain and the fourth, an approved school youth, is a house captain. These youths are likely to be passed up to the Railway Training School in Nairobi next year.[25]

In addition, John Coutts, the Minister for Education, Labour and Lands noted when he visited Wamumu on July 5, 1957 that he was most impressed with the work being done there. He observed that "there was a steady demand for graduates from this remarkable boys' town or Manyani University as had been nicknamed by some employers."[26] Attesting further to the success of Wamumu programs in reforming the detained youths, and how they had helped him discover his abilities in youth education and leadership, Gikubu noted:

> It was a wonderful rehabilitation experience. It showed me that I had a gift and talent for dealing with young people. So this was the first step on the way to what I came to do later at Starehe Boys Centre and School and I have been on it for over five decades. On the whole, Wamumu programs were good, very holistic and educative. It important to note however, that the programs did not lessen my loyalty to the Mau Mau movement.[27]

Towards the end of 1956, Wamumu continued to face the problem that it had to turn away scores of spirited youngsters and their equally enthusiastic parents, who wrote or turned up at the school gate seeking entrance. This public enthusiasm illustrates the impact that the initial educational experiences had. From the wide range of education that was offered, it is evident that Wamumu was a key launching pad for Gikubu's future engagement in Kenyan youth education. Its success gave him confidence in his abilities to manage and transform youths.

In comparison to the rest of the camps in the pipeline, Wamumu, with its proclaimed ethos of "Truth and Loyalty," was "a paradise for young Mau Mau suspects."[28] Because of the success of its programs, many Wamumu youths were also employed after their release in its parent Department of the Community Development and Rehabilitation or with settlers who were impressed with the camp's programs. It was not long before the reputation of Wamumu spread to other camps. When Colin Owen, a probation officer, went to assess the youths who were being held in such places as Manyani, he found young detainees clamoring to be selected for transfer to Wamumu, although there was not enough room for them. Hundreds of those who were arrested and imprisoned or detained as teenagers remained in the camps for several years, by which time they were too old to be transferred to Wamumu. Some of them, in an attempt to get around this, did their best to appear even younger than they were and managed to find their way to Wamumu. It was this success that led some colonial officials to refer to the camp as the "Eton of Africa." Although an exaggeration, the comparison illustrates the respect that was accorded to Wamumu's programs in colonial government circles in the 1950s.

It is critical to note that despite its success, the work of Wamumu also came under fire. Its critics asked why former criminals were receiving better treatment and education than other Kenyans who had given no trouble to the colonial government. Its programs were viewed as political propaganda. According to Paul Ocobock, the types of skills developed at Wamumu should be viewed with skepticism. While they were developing those skills, African youths were also building an institution for their own confinement, painting signs for the colonial facilities, and harvesting crops to be handed over to the state.[29] Close examination of colonial youth policies at this time indicates that the construction of African citizenry at Wamumu was less about the mindset of its former inmates than the aura the state placed around them. Although there were nine youth camps in operation after 1954 throughout Central Province, nowhere in the official public records was another camp mentioned other than in passing. As the theater of the Nairobi streets made the Kenyan public anxious, the stage on which Wamumu performed served to placate those fears. Only at Wamumu could the state take 1,200 hardened Mau Mau juveniles and transform them into employable and disciplined citizens. However, once the 1,200 were released, the Wamumu façade was washed away by the practicalities of colonial vagrancy policy.[30]

This brings to the fore the question whether Wamumu's rehabilitative and civilizing project was a success. In some ways yes, as evidenced in my earlier discussion, but what the colonial officials intended the camp to be may not have been what the youths took away from it. Wamumu and the youth camp system did indeed relieve many frustrations that had driven young men and women to join the Mau Mau War in the first place. Wamumu, Othaya, Mukurweini, and other camp inmates received education, skills training, employment, land, and a unique element of kinship with their fellow inmates. Although very basic in its educational programs, the colonial regime introduced African youths to the colonial economy and patronage network, potentially but not necessarily lessening their loyalty to the Mau Mau. Paul Ocobock observes that "Peter Mathenge, the son of Mau Mau general Stanley Mathenge, bitterly complained that being forced to leave Othaya Youth Camp would end his free education, something to which he believed he was entitled to. Despite this benefit, he was glad however, that he had great devotion to the cause of freedom than the Wamumu and Othaya programs."[31] Furthermore, it is unlikely that rehabilitation inculcated youth camp inmates with a sense of loyalty or imbued them with colonial citizenship, as the state had intended. This is evidenced in the active participation of youth in the Mau Mau movement after their release. Describing this lacuna, Gikubu noted:

Although Wamumu gave us vital life skills such as direction in life, discipline, leadership, importance of hard work that were essential to enable us navigate the socio-economic upheavals that had been thrust on us by the colonial government, the training however, did not lessen our loyalty to the Mau Mau movement. We wanted freedom. We wanted independence and we could not rest until we got these things. Wamumu hardened us further. It gave us education and light to demand our independence and more rights.[32]

Expounding further on the comments by Gikubu with regard to the effects of Wamumu programs on the detainees and their attitudes to Mau Mau movement, Caroline Elkins writes:

The Emergency camps and prisons provided a new venue for the anticolonial and civil struggle, and the Mau Mau adherents seized the initiative. Behind the wire, detainees reaffirmed their commitment to the movement and adapted battle strategies and oathing rituals to their newfound circumstances. Nairobi turned increasingly to violence and coercion to regain control over the pipeline. Government and detainees became locked in a bitter struggle. By 1956, a time when many Kenyan historians declared the insurgency well concluded, Mau Mau was raging in the Emergency detention camps and prisons while the colonial government searched for a means to re-establish its authority.[33]

An examination of other rehabilitation programs which ran on similar lines to Wamumu indicate the opposite of their intentions. For instance, legends on the gates of some of the rehabilitation camps did not reflect their rehabilitation mission. At Aguthi Camp, detainees were greeted with large letters that read "He Who Helps Himself Will Also Be Helped." Fort Hall's main camp bore a sign reading "Abandon Hope All Ye Who Enter Here."[34] These slogans hardly evoke images of the rehabilitation paradise that was being peddled by the colonial government to the media and to anticolonial critics through the Wamumu programs. There was minimal budget and manpower allocation to the program. According to Kenya's Developmental Plan at the time, the Community Development and Rehabilitation Department allocated 0.5 percent of the colony's total budget to the program. This amount was to be spent on both the Mau Mau rehabilitation program and other community development projects throughout Kenya. Owing to the scant financial support that the rehabilitation program received, in order to keep the program afloat Askwith sought financial help from other departments and outside donors. There was no indication of the colonial government's dedication to the program. Successful implementation of the rehabilitation program would have required a complete shift in the public's perception of Mau Mau, the authoritarian nature of the British colonial government, and its plans for continued imperial domination in Kenya's post-Emergency future, something the colonial government was not prepared to do. Giving a comprehensive examination of the lack of support for rehabilitation in some colonial government quarters, Caroline Elkins writes:

> Askwith's plans for sweeping reforms had little chance of being implemented in the late colonial Kenya, and certainly not during the Emergency's escalating chaos and authoritarianism. Even had there been abroad consensus of support for his program, the circumstances would have rendered its implementation difficult at best. Budgetary constraints, staffing difficulties and the demands of repatriation, screening and ultimately detention together stretched the colonial government as never before. These practical challenges then collided with-and were accentuated by-an increasing conservatism among the colony's decision-makers, and the loyalist community more broadly. From the start, rehabilitation hardly elicited widespread support, even from Kenya's liberal minority. Yet this skepticism over reform grew and was replaced by a hard-line demand for retribution and control. The shift towards authoritarianism was, in part, a response to the government's inability to control events. Indeed, government action – whether undertaken by European or African agents often inflamed civil and anti-colonial antagonisms and further catalyzed support for the insurgency.[35]

It is important to note that despite several failures and challenges that were witnessed in the rehabilitation program, the colonial government used every opportunity to highlight its success, as was seen in the case of Wamumu as a way of achieving its civilizing agenda. Whenever colonial officials were accused of torture or misconduct in detention camps or in emergency villages, they tactically used the success of the rehabilitation as the mitigation tool to rationalize the situation. Apart from a handful of humane and reform-minded colonial officers who worked in the pipeline, rehabilitation was not evident in the camps or barbed-wire villages of colonial Kenya. With the camps filling up and public criticism mounting, Benjamin Korir notes that "the colonial government would not deviate from its misleading rhetoric, deliberately extolling as a legitimating ideology in order to mask the increasing violence and brutality of detention without trial in Kenya."[36]

Whether the training, discipline, and education at Wamumu had left an indelible mark on the majority of inmates is unknown and is a matter of debate, as evidenced from the scanty colonial literature on the larger operations of most of the colonial rehabilitation programs. What is clear, however, as earlier discussed in this chapter, is that the colonial government took great pride in Wamumu graduates, their work, and performance after their release. A report visit by the Secretary for Community Development to Wamumu in 1956 affirms this pride. In his letter to Gardner after the visit, he expressed his delight at Wamumu's success and the need to link its rehabilitation work to the larger Kenyan colony. He noted: "I was very pleased with all that you showed us on our recent visit to Wamumu. Since coming back it has occurred to me that it might be of assistance to you and good for the boys if you could share their success in the colony."[37]

Another example that illustrates the pride of colonial government in Wamumu programs is evidenced in the recommendation letter by Austen Albu, a representative from the office of Alan Lennox-Boyd, the Secretary of State for the Colonies in Britain, who after his visit to Wamumu on 2nd April, 1958 recommended the need for the House of Commons to honor Gardner for his great work at Wamumu. He urged the House of Commons to conduct a research study on the reasons behind the camp's success and how the findings could be replicated in other British colonies. In his communication, he wrote:

> While in Kenya, we were very much impressed by the youths' rehabilitation school at Wamumu. The work that is being done here is really quite astounding and I do think that some recognition of the commandant, Capt. George Gardner, is overdue. It would also, I think, be of great interest to have a serious research study made of what, in fact, has happened to these youths and the reasons for the success of the school. This might have relevance both for the rehabilitation of Mau Mau in general, and the problems of juvenile delinquency, not only in Africa but in our other colonies. I believe it would not be difficult, if the Colonial Office were to set an enquiry afoot, to obtain funds from an American research foundation which supports the social sciences, for this purpose.[38]

To illustrate further its pride in Wamumu's programs, the colonial government requested its Principal Probation Officer and Chief Inspector of Approved Schools to contact the Wamumu management for a write-up and news coverage on its progress and success, as attested by this letter: "the

Information Department wish to arrange to visit the camp for the above mentioned purpose and to demonstrate the work that is being done by you and your staff. Both Askwith and myself feel it would be a good thing to show the public your great work."[39]

Although the Wamumu camp was a success to a great extent and served its immediate purpose of reforming young detainees, who in the first place should not have been detained, it was not suited to those youths who joined the school in later years. Instead of the hardcore ex-Mau Mau youths, the school began to get street youths and truants. Any youth who was caught loitering in the streets or was thought to be a deviant was taken to Wamumu. At the start of 1957, Gardner and his associates at Wamumu faced a swollen inmate population. More youths were matriculating into rehabilitation than those graduating from it, and most were not charged with Mau Mau involvement. Scores of orphans, juvenile criminals, and child laborers without passes were being transferred by district commissioners and screening teams from Kikuyu reserves to Wamumu. This is succinctly affirmed by Gardner in the following communication about the increasing levels of the so called "orphans" juvenile category at Wamumu. In his communication to the District Officer, Embu Division on May 13, 1958, he wrote:

> I am returning herewith the 2 orphans together with their committal orders. I regret that I am unable to admit them. I have already been forced to accept so many youths on Approved School Orders, owing to a lack of other accommodation for them, that the school is already 121 boys over strength. I will contact you in the event of vacancies occurring in the future. Unfortunately it would appear that in the past Embu Divisions have sent here a good many boys who in fact are not genuine orphans. This has occurred through youths themselves making false statements, and in some cases, I regret, through African headmen and village authorities condoning a child's false pretense to enter Wamumu. The plan is to first sort out what we have, if necessary returning to their homes the culprits, and thereafter to tighten up on the method of committal.[40]

While amazed that "hardened terrorists" could be transformed into fine employees within two years or less, Wamumu administrators realized that the more ex-Mau Mau suspects they released the more the cost and merit of the camp came under scrutiny. With more and more bed spaces available, they were being filled with a diversity of juvenile inmates from "waifs, strays and orphans" to upper-class Kikuyus. According to KNA AB/4/44 Report, William Mosley, Community Development Officer in charge of Mukurweini, the Mau Mau youths only accounted for 50 percent of the inmate population. Community Development officials began to complain to the provincial administration that Wamumu as a youth camp and approved institution could only house youths in need of "care and protection" as stipulated under the Emergency Regulations Act. They argued that administrators in Nairobi and in the provinces were using Wamumu as a dumping ground for unruly youths rather than using Juvenile Reception Centres (JRCs) and approved schools. As a result of this, the Department of Community Development was under intense pressure from the Treasury Department to reduce the cost and population of Wamumu. This meant speeding up the process of rehabilitation of the Mau Mau youth. To accomplish this, the Department of Community Development needed to halt the number of juveniles being transferred from the JRC to Wamumu. It also called for the revocation of Government Notice No. 16/55 and to rely on the Prevention of Cruelty and Neglect of Children Ordinance for future committals to Wamumu. This procedure was meant to ensure a very thorough investigation of each case before a committal order was made, and also to enable the magistrate to order the parents to contribute towards the maintenance of youth who were committed to Wamumu. It is important to note that the capacity of Wamumu grew rapidly during this time and that Gardner was gravely concerned about this, declining to take in more inmates. In order to address the Wamumu overpopulation problem and other youth challenges, the Department of Community Development was urged to utilize JRCs as sieving mechanisms for youths who were in need of great care. The following section discusses the role that JRCs played in this regard.

ROLE OF JRCs IN ADDRESSING WAMUMU'S OVERPOPULATION AND YOUTH VAGRANCY CHALLENGES

In order to address the increase of youth vagrancy and other challenges, colonial officials began drawing up plans in early 1957 for a series of JRCs in Kiambu, Fort Hall, and Nyeri districts which were meant to operate as "sorting houses" from which the youths could be channeled to appropriate institutions, such as approved schools, mission schools, youth camps, youths' villages, and homes. The JRCs were originally conceived as "places of safety" under the Emergency Regulations Act of 1954. This was mainly a funding consideration: as "places of safety" they could use the government's own funds given to the provincial administration or funds from the coffers of the Emergency Community Development. At its simplest, the JRC was a holding and transit camp for juveniles of all sorts who had been repatriated by the state. The Emergency had relied so heavily on repatriation as a means of removing Africans en masse that juveniles were being removed from multiple locations throughout Kenya. The JRCs provided a badly needed transition structure for a chaotic colonial process that handled youth vagrancy.[41]

JRCs were opened in major districts of Central Province such as Kiambu, Nyeri, and Fort Hall. But unlike Wamumu, within two years they ran into financial difficulties. As more and more juveniles were removed from various areas throughout Kenya, transportation costs begun to mount. In 1957, the probation services, which were in charge of repatriations out of Nairobi and other areas and into the JRCs, according to the KNA OP/1/1017 Report by Barry Riseborough, Permanent Secretary for Community Development to Provincial Commissioner, Central Province, in 1957 the emergency traveling expenses were estimated as having to increase by 60 percent because of the number of juveniles who had to be repatriated to the JRCs. Despite these financial woes, the government did all it could to keep the JRC system functioning. By 1959, the state was dependent on the JRCs for holding and repatriating urban as well as rural juvenile vagrants.[42] According to the KNA OP/1/1017 Report, Richard Wilkinson, the officer in charge, worried that if the JRC system was dismantled there would be no control over the return of repatriates. When the Emergency Regulations Act was repealed in 1960 and funding for the JRCs was in jeopardy, they were regazetted as remand homes, falling under the financial jurisdiction of the colonial government according to the newly introduced Vagrancy Ordinance of 1960. This ordinance in conjunction with other youth-related laws enabled the colonial state to maintain the institutions it had developed to exert greater control over Kenya's youth.[43]

The establishment of JRCs was not sufficient to address youth vagrancy during this period. Simply holding suspected vagrants and criminals in massive pens consisting of four foot high barbed wire and an open entrance could not prevent the recidivist vagrant from returning to Nairobi.[44] Investigating where inmates lived, which families they belonged to, and how to transport them there took time, especially if those held were urban youths whose homes were back in the cities from which they were removed. One key question in the early days of JRCs was how the colonial officials could keep the inmates busy. As a result, the JRCs developed in conjunction with another mechanism of control that was developed by the state in the waning days of the Mau Mau: youth clubs. Chapter 4 discusses at length the role that youth clubs played in this process.

The JRCs were an extension of previous colonial policies regarding juvenile vagrants and delinquents. They aimed to provide colonial officials with centralized and efficient mechanisms for controlling youth movements within the colony. Despite the fact that the Kiambu and Fort Hall JRCs were fulfilling their function as sorting houses, they fell far short of their expectations. The district commissioners and community development officers could not agree on the precise function of JRCs. The situation was due, in part, to a shared jurisdiction of the centers between Community Development and the Provincial Administration. Here conservative and liberal mindsets were in conflict. The district commissioner of Kiambu believed that the JRC was a wholly penal institution, whereas community development officials such as Barry Riseborough argued that JRCs were merely sorting houses. Paradoxically, both visions of the JRC system operated in tandem throughout the State of Emergency, resulting in neglect and maltreatment of the youth. This showed the deplorable state of the colonial care and protection policy for youths during this period.[45]

There is limited historical record about the lives that the youth led in transit camps or in JRCs. What is known is that investigations into the antecedents of the juveniles undertaken by the colonial district commissioners and community development officers took a great deal of time: the sorting system was slow, complex, and very confusing. The records show that in 1959 juveniles were in remand in JRCs for periods as long as 75 and 99 days. Their lives during these months spent idly behind the wire were not pleasant. For instance, the juvenile and Mau Mau adults were not separated; boys and girls mingled and slept together. There were no solid floors in the large sheds in which they slept, and because of the rains the entire camp was a seething mass of mud.[46] The youths had nothing to do but sit around in filthy clothes. They not only had a dilapidated environment to endure but also physical abuse. In 1958, according to the KNA VQ/21/2 Report, Griffin observed that corporal punishment was being used to an inordinate extent in some JRCs. This demonstrates the competing visions for the centers from the Provincial Administration and community development officers. The Provincial Administration viewed many of the juveniles passing through their JRCs as delinquents who were in need of discipline.

Throughout 1957 and early 1958, the JRCs were run on a punitive basis, and the young people vehemently opposed their mistreatment. This was clearly evidenced in the several cases of juvenile escapes in Fort Hall and Kiambu.[47]

Despite the appalling conditions and physical punishment, the JRCs continued to operate as "sorting houses." Roundups, repatriations, and detention became the primary vehicles for juvenile control in the late Emergency period. The "juvenile pipeline" allowed colonial officials to more precisely extract Mau Mau suspects, Emergency orphans, juvenile criminals, and migratory casual laborers from the population and to transfer them to a variety of institutions developed to manage them. While the JRCs separated youths from adults and systematized the state's control over youth, conditions behind the wire were no less traumatic. It is true that community development and the Provincial Administration made no grand claims that the JRCs were to involve a rehabilitative mission; only late in the Emergency period were there moves to incorporate rehabilitation into the JRCs.[48] Rehabilitation was to take place within the institutions that the JRCs linked to the growing influx of uncontrolled juvenile migrants; places such as mission schools, approved schools, youth camps, and the newly added conduit in the juvenile pipeline: the rural youth club.

It is vital to note that any holes that the Secretary of Defence had in his system were plugged by simply shifting juvenile vagrants and other youths from one institution to another until overcrowding required another move. An example that affirms this is evidenced in the KNA/WAMYOU/SEC/POL/32 Wamumu Approved School report of 1957, in which of the 125 youths who were sent to their homes in Embu, 70 were offered employment upon completion of training and 50 were sent to either Kabete or Dagoretti approved schools. Wamumu in Embu District and Mukuruweini in Nyeri District, because they had more facilities, took the bulk of these juveniles. In both places, there were juveniles who were detained under the State of Emergency Regulations, those who committed criminal offenses and were being held at the governor's pleasure, those sentenced to approved schools, and those classified as waifs, strays, and orphans. All of them were repatriated back to their reserves via the youth camp program.

Throughout 1957, Wamumu exemplified the chaotic nature of the State of Emergency policies concerning juveniles. Rather than solve the juvenile problem by repatriating thousands of juveniles back to the reserves and containing them there, it complicated a set of procedures that took two decades to sort out. Overcrowding led to the confinement of a cornucopia of categorized juveniles within the same institution.[49] Yet while Wamumu was in a period of flux, officials began to find a firm footing and a structured way to control African youth. Although Owles and Griffin were convinced that the street waifs needed a lesser dose of rehabilitation, Gardner was convinced otherwise. Slowly, the administrative differences between Griffin and Owles on one side and Gardner on the other forced Wamumu to close down. Roger Martin argues that there was only one cohort of "terrorists" from the detention camps, and that as they were released the vacant places were filled by youths, sometimes only eight years old, who had been committed by the courts but whose only "offence" was to be in need of care and protection. Youths like this required a different system of reform program than the tough discipline of Wamumu, a change that Gardner was not ready to embrace. He was very conservative, insisting that the new youths should be subjected to the same form of severe rehabilitation procedures as those who had been rescued from Manyani Detention Camp. Owles and Griffin were convinced that they needed a different form of rehabilitation because they were not hardened criminals. The tension emanating from this threatened to tear the camp apart. Commenting on this administrative impasse, Roger Martin observes:

> The tough, unyielding discipline and active occupation of every waking hour which had made Wamumu famous was, however, the only system Gardner could understand. A Manyani detainee looking forward to early release could be philosophical if Gardner flogged him, stripped him, shaved him or made him wear a placard on his neck reading "MBWA" (dog). He could endure solitary confinement in a tiny cell without too much distress. But the young children who failed to sweep their dormitory properly, chatted in church or lost their clothes, were treated with identical severity, so that the morale of the school declined and they became inexplicably but genuinely ill. Griffin and Owles understood the situation but were powerless to correct it, save by running down the numbers in the school while Gardner was away on leave through short "corrective courses."[50]

It was clear by 1958 that the threat from Mau Mau youths had been neutralized. The issue at hand concerned the hundreds of youths who were being arrested in Nairobi and throughout Central Province for criminal acts, vagrancy, and pass law infractions. Although by 1958 the days of rehabilitating Mau Mau youths were over, the rehabilitation of young criminals had just begun. Accordingly, Wamumu and its sister camps underwent legal and functional changes. Wamumu and the camp at Othaya were regazetted as approved schools and joined Kabete and Dagoreti in their task of managing criminal and delinquent youths. The name was changed from Wamumu Rehabilitation Camp to Wamumu Approved School in 1960.

OTHAYA APPROVED SCHOOL

With the closure of Wamumu, Gikubu, owing to his superb leadership skills, was taken up by Roger Owles to help take care of the young boys at Othaya Approved School. He joined the school on June 6, 1958 and worked there until June 9, 1959. Owles felt that with Gikubu at his side it was going to be easy for him to run the school. Recalling his acceptance to join Owles after his release from Wamumu, Gikubu noted: "I had worked closely with Owles at both Manyani and Wamumu. I knew him very well and I loved his character and work ethic. I knew I could make a difference in the lives of the youths under his care."[51] So while his other inmates were released to their respective villages and homes, Gikubu went to Othaya Approved School to help Owles in his work. After it had been gazetted, Othaya was taken over by District Commissioner Nyeri on behalf of the provincial commissioner and was run as an approved institution for the province. It was expected to take the place of Wamumu under the Emergency Regulations Act of 1954. The officer in charge was expected to be someone in whose care children in need of help and protection could be committed. Youths were only admitted on committal orders by a competent authority. Because of financial reasons only a maximum of 300 could be accommodated at the institution. Admission was normally through the JRC mechanism if it existed in the area. The responsibility for adequate investigation and documentation of cases to be admitted to Othaya School was placed on JRC staff and Gikubu. They were assisted in their work by local community development officers, probation officers, and provincial administration officials.

The gazetting of Othaya as an approved school allowed Wamumu to finally relieve itself of the juveniles who had been charged with criminal offences. Since the closure of Save the Children Fund Home at Ujana Park, Othaya Approved School was the only residential institution of its kind in Kenya at the time, and it was a happy place throughout its short existence. In 1960, despite all the efforts of its supporters, it was turned into an approved school owing to a lack of funds to maintain its initial mission and the inability of African district councils within Nyeri Province to meet much of its cost. On its closure, the buildings, equipment, and management were moved from the Office of the Commissioner of Kenya Prisons to the Office of the Commissioner for Community Development and Rehabilitation. This allowed Wamumu to undergo its final colonial transformation, as an intermediate approved school managing juveniles between the ages of 13 and 15. As an approved school, its function lay in managing juvenile delinquents and some recidivist vagrants. Its days as a means of constructing productive citizens out of counterproductive Mau Mau adherents were over. Owles lost his command and the chance to put his wise and compassionate attitudes about childcare into practice. Griffin, on the other hand, was more fortunate. Late in 1957, while still fully engrossed in Wamumu's work, he was requested by his commissioner to become the colony youth organizer, a newly created post. From 1957 onward, the state focused its attention more on repatriating vagrants and delinquents out of Nairobi back to rural areas.

Othaya Approved School allowed Owles to put his childcare skills into practice. He found a strong right hand in Gikubu. Othaya Approved School operated like a normal school, offering a variety of trades. Gikubu's work was similar to his earlier work at Wamumu with a few additional roles. He was the student leader in charge of the entire school, and he had more authority and responsibilities than at Wamumu, also being in charge of discipline and the junior school. In addition, he assisted in the screening of youths who wanted to join the school. Gikubu's skills in youth education and leadership were greatly refined at Othaya. He observed that:

> It was at Othaya that I cut my teeth in youth education. I knew I could make a difference through assisting youths to get a good education. I loved working with the young people. Their success in our various programs delighted my heart. I knew I could do anything with them. I engaged in various leadership roles at Othaya than I had done at Wamumu. We worked very well with Owles and we offered more trade and educational courses to the youths. It was very rewarding work.[52]

On the whole, through the work of Wamumu Rehabilitation Camp, this chapter demonstrates in detail the rehabilitation programs that were undertaken by the colonial government, various programs that were offered in them, and the political propaganda and controversies that were entailed in the process. The chapter illustrates in depth how the rehabilitation programs that were undertaken during this period reflect a lack of coherent colonial programs on youth education and vagrancy. In addition, the chapter raises fundamental questions about colonizer and colonized relations during the colonial period. The relationships that developed between Griffin, Gikubu, and Geturo, and the change of heart that the former developed for the latter two, brings to the fore the often underresearched relationships that existed between colonizer and colonized, and the good that was demonstrated by the colonizer as seen in the case of Griffin, Gardner, and Owles at Wamumu, as well as how the process came full circle at SBC. The reciprocity of the colonized, as shown by Gikubu's work with Griffin and Owles, illustrates how roses were able to bloom from the thorns that existed during the colonial period. The power of the union between the two is clearly depicted in the success of Wamumu's programs, and later the foundation of SBC, as will be discussed in Chap. 4. It is important to underscore that there is limited scholarship to shed light on these relations, hence the essence of this work is discerning these relationships, the underlying colonial policies, and the social, cultural, educational, political, and economic lessons that emerge from them. The chapter accentuates that an in-depth examination of Gikubu's educational engagements and activities at Wamumu and Othaya demonstrates that the two camps indeed sharpened his skills in youth education. The two institutions gave him the opportunity to lead students, create, participate, and nurture new academic and cocurricular programs. It was at these institutions that he was able to enhance his passion and acumen in youth education and leadership. They gave him valuable lessons, encouragement, and conviction in youth education and leadership that enabled him to develop SBC to great heights.

Notes

1. A communication KNA/WAMYOU/G/20/13 from Captain George Gardner, the officer in charge of Wamumu, to Thomas Askwith, the Commissioner for Community Development and Rehabilitation, dated October 11, 1955 on the official title of Wamumu.
2. Interview, Joseph Gikubu, August 11, 2012.
3. Television Interview, Geoffrey Griffin, October 2000.
4. A communication KNA/WAMYOU/G/6/28 from George Gardner to the Commissioner for Community Development and Rehabilitation dated September 28, 1955 detailing the various heinous activities of the 32 hardcore youths at Wamumu in the early days.

5. Roger Martin, *Anthem of Bugles: The Story of Starehe Boys Centre and School* (Nairobi: Heinemann Educational Books Ltd., 1978), 16.
6. Yusuf King'ala, *The Autobiography of Geoffrey William Griffin: Kenya's Champion Beggar* (Nairobi: Falcon Crest, 2005), 50.
7. King'ala, *The Autobiography of Geoffrey William Griffin: Kenya's Champion Beggar*, 51.
8. George Gardner's inaugural speech to the youths when they arrived at Wamumu covered by the Standard Newspaper in 1956 on the purpose of the Wamumu rehabilitation program.
9. Interview, Geoffrey Griffin, August 5, 2004.
10. Interview, Geoffrey Griffin, August 6, 2004.
11. King'ala, *The Autobiography of Geoffrey William Griffin: Kenya's Champion Beggar*, 26.
12. Kennedy Hongo and Jesse Mugambi, *Starehe Boys Centre: School and Institute. The First Forty Years 1959–1999* (Nairobi: Acton Publishers, 2003), 28.
13. A monthly report KNA/WAMYOU/G/21/92 by George Gardner to the Principal Probation Officer on Wamumu Old Boys Society and reunions dated June 6, 1956.
14. Hongo and Mugambi, *Starehe Boys Centre: School and Institute. The First Forty Years 1959–1999*, 30.
15. Ibid.
16. Ibid., 26.
17. Documentary Interview, Geoffrey Griffin, September 4, 2004.
18. Gardner's report KNA/WAMYOU/G/21/92 that credits Wamumu's success to his officers and Gikubu's leadership prowess.
19. Caroline Elkins, *Imperial Reckoning: The Untold Story of Britain's Gulag in Kenya* (New York: Henry Holt and Company, 2005).
20. Paul Ocobock, "Joy Rides for Juveniles: Vagrant Youth and Colonial Control in Nairobi, Kenya, 1901–1952," *Social History*, 31.1(2006): 39–59.
21. Ocobock, "Joy Rides for Juveniles: Vagrant Youth and Colonial Control in Nairobi, Kenya, 1901–1952".
22. Ibid.
23. Elkins, *Imperial Reckoning: The Untold Story of Britain's Gulag in Kenya*, 210.
24. King'ala, *The Autobiography of Geoffrey William Griffin: Kenya's Champion Beggar*, 55.
25. Weekly Digest Magazine in 1957, attesting to Wamumu's excellence in scouting, 6.
26. Mr. John Coutts, the then Minister for Education, Labour, and Lands, when he visited Wamumu on July 5, 1957, impressions of the great educational work that was being done at the institution.
27. Interview, Joseph Gikubu, August 25, 2013.

28. Elkins, *Imperial Reckoning: The Untold Story of Britain's Gulag in Kenya*, 215.
29. Ocobock, "Joy Rides for Juveniles: Vagrant Youth and Colonial Control in Nairobi, Kenya, 1901–1952".
30. Ibid.
31. Ibid., 11.
32. Interview, Joseph Gikubu, August 2, 2013.
33. Atieno Odhiambo and John Lonsdale, *Mau Mau and Nationhood: Arms, Authority and Narration* (Athens: Ohio University Press, 2003), 206.
34. Peter Ojiambo, *Teaching Beyond Teaching: Geoffrey William Griffin and Starehe Boys Centre and School* (Saarbrucken, Germany: VDM Verlag, 2008), 229.
35. Odhiambo and Lonsdale, *Mau Mau and Nationhood: Arms, Authority and Narration*, 203.
36. Benjamin Kipkorir, *Biographical Essays on Imperialism and Colonialism in Colonial Kenya* (Nairobi: Kenya Literature Bureau, 1980), 119–120.
37. A report KNA/CRD/ADM/61/60 on the visit by the acting Secretary for Community Development to Wamumu in 1956 affirming the colonial government pride of Wamumu's success and the need to link its rehabilitation work to the larger Kenyan colony.
38. A recommendation letter by Austen Albu, KNA/APPR/PUB/1/1/1/25, a representative from the office of Alan Lennox-Boyd, the Secretary of State for the Colonies in Britain, who after his visit to Wamumu dated April 2, 1958 recommended the need for the House of Commons to honor George Gardner for his great work at Wamumu. He urged the House of Commons to conduct a research study into the reasons behind Wamumu's success and how the findings could be replicated in other British colonies.
39. A request KNA/APPR/PUB/1/1/1/25 by the colonial government to its principal probation officer and chief inspector of approved schools dated January 3, 1956 to contact Wamumu management for a write-up and news coverage to highlight its progress and success.
40. A communication KNA/WAMYOU/G/29/329 from George Gardner to District Officer, Embu Division on the increased levels of "orphans" juvenile category at Wamumu dated May 13, 1958.
41. Ojiambo, *Teaching Beyond Teaching: Geoffrey William Griffin and Starehe Boys Centre and School*.
42. Ibid.
43. Benjamin Kipkorir, *Biographical Essays on Imperialism and Colonialism in Colonial Kenya*.
44. Ibid.
45. Ibid.

46. Ocobock, "Joy Rides for Juveniles: Vagrant Youth and Colonial Control in Nairobi, Kenya, 1901–1952".
47. Ojiambo, *Teaching Beyond Teaching: Geoffrey William Griffin and Starehe Boys Centre and School.*
48. Ibid.
49. Atieno Odhiambo and John Lonsdale, *Mau Mau and Nationhood: Arms, Authority and Narration* (Athens: Ohio University Press, 2003), 206.
50. Martin, *Anthem of Bugles: The Story of Starehe Boys Centre and School*, 17.
51. Interview, Joseph Gikubu, August 2, 2013.August 2, 2013.
52. Benjamin Kipkorir, *Biographical Essays on Imperialism and Colonialism in Colonial Kenya.*

CHAPTER 4

Called to Educate: Kariokor and Starehe Youth Clubs

Gikubu's full involvement in Kenyan youth education is epitomized in the formation of youth clubs that were a precursor to Starehe Boys Centre and School (SBC). In order to understand this involvement, it is imperative to examine the formation of youth clubs, their aims, objectives, and role in curbing youth vagrancy in Nairobi and later in Kenya at large. Between 1947 and 1949, there were increasing levels of youth vagrancy in Nairobi. Amidst the postwar population growth of Nairobi and the increasing poverty and crime there, mass roundups and repatriation continued to be the mechanisms for managing the city's underemployed, especially youths. By this time, many officials within the colonial government were certain that repatriation was a long-term failure that resulted in "continued vagrancy."[1] However, they perceived no alternative strategy. Although some colonial administrators believed that there were more important issues than juvenile discipline, others sought long-term solutions that would eliminate juvenile delinquency and vagabondage.[2] During this period, there were huge numbers of African children who could neither access nor afford education. Very little existed by way of secondary education and there was a virtual ban on the creation of new secondary schools. As a consequence, child vagrancy begun to assume alarming proportions, and there was fear within the colonial government that the youth problem was becoming as dangerous as the Mau Mau movement. There was an urgent need to address the matter. What was needed was a chain of schools to provide full-time occupation. Although the word "school" could not be used, institutions

© The Author(s) 2017
P.O. Ojiambo, *Kenyan Youth Education in Colonial and Post-Colonial Times*, Historical Studies in Education,
DOI 10.1007/978-3-319-59990-8_4

could be created under the name of "youth clubs" or "youth centres." These would concentrate on technical and agricultural programs that were deemed beneficial to African rural development.

In 1957, the Juvenile Employment Committee met in Nairobi to discuss ways in which the underemployed youth of the city could be put to work. Committee members openly expressed their dismay that despite the State of Emergency regulations nothing was preventing juveniles from undertaking the trek back to Nairobi. In fact, the number of repatriations was increasing, with the Nairobi District Commissioner reporting that he was removing 400 juveniles from the city each month. Committee members had no idea how many youths were residing in Nairobi without permanent employment, yet they believed that idle youths were continuing to commit crimes, although providing them with jobs would either come into conflict with labor regulations or would result in adult unemployment. As the Juvenile Employment Committee grumbled about urban youth, two new mechanisms were being developed under the auspices of the Welfare of Children Regulations that would attempt to solve repatriation's inadequacies and challenges: Juvenile Reception Centres (JRCs) and youth clubs. These were developed to keep African youth occupied in the rural areas once they were repatriated. Drawing on some of the programs used in approved schools and the youth camp programs, the JRCs and youth clubs became part of the state's long-awaited response to increasing urban vagrancy.[3]

In Britain during the Second World War, notions of citizenship were raised with respect to young people, driven partly by concerns about loyalty. Organizations such as the Empire Youth Movement promoted the idea of youth as disciplined and productive members of the British Empire who could defend it against fascism and communism.[4] Similar concerns were expressed in colonial Africa. Drawing examples from British developments that addressed the problem, two Kenyan settlers, Patrick Williams and Olga Watkins, endeavored to develop youth clubs in each of the colony's districts. These would provide African youths with instruction in agriculture, manufacturing, and character training. Williams and Watkins's plans quickly broke down. A lack of interest on the part of Africans and the financial constraints of the colony led to their swift demise. However, notions about African youth were clearly changing. Europeans in the colony were beginning to believe that they could provide the moral and technical instruction that ethnic affiliations had failed to foster among urban and semi-urban juveniles. The one site where this could be accomplished was the classroom. At the end of the 1940s, officials were arguing that improvements in African education were necessary. A ten-year plan drafted in 1948 recommended that the number of teachers and students should be doubled and that financing for urban schools should be increased. But the committees researching the deficiencies of African education did not stop with a call for more staff and facilities but rather sought to alter the nature of education itself. In their view, African children required training in civics and citizenship. It was with this conceptualization of African education that the Beecher Report recommended the permeation of the right attitudes toward society into every aspect of school life.[5]

Education, just like the transfer of the African family from the farm to the city, provided another set of disciplinary tools to keep African youth off the streets. In their report on Education for Citizenship in Africa, the colonial officials revealed their anxieties over urbanizing youth. The state advocated the introduction of Western civilization to the colonies and controlling its impact on the people. To do this, the regime turned to the education of citizens using its own design. The goal was no longer to reconnect youths to their "traditional" values but rather to equip them with vital skills that could enable them to tackle unfamiliar tasks that were imposed on them by modern life, with the hope of "civilizing them." By the early 1950s, the work of various committees revealed that perceptions about African youth among many colonial officials had changed. Paul Ocobock notes that it seemed the colony was poised to alter its relationship with youth and was ready to embark on a mission of modernity. Had momentum built around the assorted reports and their recommendations, the declaration of the State of Emergency would have been prevented.[6] The emergence of the Mau Mau and the violence of the early 1950s confirmed the fears of many British officials that Africans were unable to cope with the pressures of Western civilization. And as the colonial state was strengthened under the State of Emergency, many of the failed attempts at control of the 1930s and 1940s were resuscitated.

While the Department of Community Development touted the rehabilitation of juvenile Mau Mau suspects and delinquents at its youth camps and the systematization of repatriation through JRCs, the youth still defied State of Emergency movement orders. In 1957 and 1958, officials believed that the pipeline had slowed the movement of young people, but had increased the level of recidivism. District commissioners and community development officers began to see the same faces passing through the JRCs several times. As the youths were released back to their home reserves, many returned to a radically altered environment, in some cases to completely new villages with friends and family completely absent. Villagization and land consolidation, called for under the Swynerton Plan, had been designed to cut off the Mau Mau from their rural supply hubs.[7] As of October 1955, the government had constructed 854 villages in Central Province and forcibly moved one million Kikuyus, Merus, and Embus into them. Within these villages, the state hoped to exercise greater social control. These villagers could be more easily punished or rewarded for their participation in or abstention from the conflict. With tens of thousands of Kikuyus detained, young men and women returned to shattered domestic households held together by mothers and female kin who, between forced labor and household work, had to find the means to support their families. According to KNA AB/2/62 Report, Fort Hall women in Kandara Division went out to pick coffee on daily or monthly contracts and had to leave their children at home because their employers did not want the children brought along. Visitors to the villages complained that the compounds were solely occupied by children, most of whom had various illnesses. Without families, education, or employment in the villages, young people were further thrust into the criminal underworld.[8]

While Eileen Fletcher's exposé and the findings of the missions shocked the British public, her findings would not have come as a surprise to colonial officials in Kenya. The Ministry of Community Development had explored solutions to juvenile migration and rural upheaval well before Fletcher's report was released in 1957. The ministry decided to develop a series of youth clubs throughout Central Province in order to occupy children who were without schooling, delinquent youths in need of reform, and those who were poor.

AIMS AND ACTIVITIES OF YOUTH CLUBS

In 1957, the first pilot clubs were developed in Nyeri District. Mathira was chosen as an experimental location by the government because it had been deeply infected by the Mau Mau and was a hotbed of sedition. The clubs began in October 1956 and by the end of that year there were 17 of them in Mathira Division, and 44 in Nyeri District. They were expected to spread to other districts. It was realized from the beginning that the scheme should be based on a voluntary effort on the part of the people rather than a compulsory one imposed by the government. For several months, community development officers, such as Don Diment and Peter Moll, had discussed the project with local chiefs, and their cooperation was quickly secured.

Within a year each of the chiefs had obtained five acres of land from their communities, using "carrot and stick" methods, and had built a large clubhouse of mud and wattle with a thatched roof on each site. The willingness of the people to help was shown by the fact that £3,600 was soon contributed by them. It is important to note that Moll and Diment had started local youth club schemes of their own earlier, and Griffin had been very impressed with them when he made his tour of Nyeri upon being appointed colony youth organizer. He felt there was a need to expand the idea to the entire province, and later throughout Kenya.

The clubs aimed to provide village youths with activities of a useful and instructive nature, together with sporting and cultural pastimes, with a view to broadening their outlook and interests in life. Additionally, they sought to teach better and more advanced agricultural methods as a way of increasing interest in the land as a means of livelihood, turning thoughts away from the white collar jobs which many youths sought during this period. Further, they sought to mold youths' thinking about their role in community development. Peter Moll gives the following summary of various activities of the youth clubs in Mathira Division, Nyeri District, when they were formed in August 1956:

> The clubs were to be established on permanent five acre plots which are being set aside for this purpose under the present land consolidation as many villages as is feasible and the membership will be drawn eventually from various villages. On each of these plots is to be built a clubhouse. Pitches for all ball games and a football field will be leveled and the remaining land is to be used as gardens and livestock pens. Activities of the youth clubs will include various sports, physical training, music, plays, concerts, lectures on agriculture, health, hygiene, civics, practical agriculture, livestock farming, domestic science, film shows, brick making, and handicrafts.[9]

An old Kikuyu custom was adopted in order to help the clubs combat the problem of misfits and ne'er-do-wells who drifted to the towns to seek employment for which they were not qualified. For their motto, the youth clubs in Mathira Division took the phrase *Iganda Ciu Riu* (modern civilization). Among the Kikuyu the clubs were places where young men and women could receive advice and knowledge that fitted them for adult life. The aim of the clubs in this regard was therefore to help young people fit into rural society with enthusiasm and industry, and become in due course good citizens of Kenya. The clubs met on three mornings a week, with a varied and instructive program having been worked out. Broadly speaking, the youth clubs kept African youths active in four principal ways: through skills training, education, entertainment, and sports. For boys, classes in carpentry, signwriting, agriculture, and leatherwork provided opportunities to develop skills they could later use in the labor market and in their daily lives. For girls, instruction was provided in home economics, cooking, sewing, dressmaking, and other skills that could keep them firmly fixed within the household.[10] Together both boys and girls were given classes in literacy, hygiene, agriculture, health, local government, and general knowledge of citizenship. Singing, sports, and dancing were a large part of the youth club activities. There was a uniform, and a badge that had two symbols: a spear and a hoe. The spear represented the primary objective of the clubs—to defend youth from evil influence—and the hoe represented the practical work of the clubs—to improve agriculture. It was clear to the colonial government that the Mathira experiment was a success, and popular, and the community development officers and other government officials put much work in it. The clubs were seen as filling the gap for Kikuyu youth who, for one reason or another, were unable to go on to an intermediate school on completion of primary education. The youth clubs were also warmly welcomed by African parents, many of whom were conscious of youths' real need for guidance.[11]

It is essential to note that there were several debates within the Ministry of Community Development on which clubs were to be used as pilot schemes—the Mathira or Othaya clubs. Griffin preferred the Othaya clubs since he had trained most of their leaders at Wamumu and was certain about their leadership capabilities. He argued in his communication to the District Community Development Officer, Nyeri District, dated September 6, 1957 that:

> I doubt if Mathira Division should be regarded as a pilot scheme area at all. An area where the leaders have not been trained by me, nor are personally known to me, should in no circumstances be looked upon as a pilot scheme for the whole organization. Without any way of depreciating the work of Mathira Community Development Officer, I personally regard the clubs there as much less promising than those in Othaya where considerable care and forethought is being exercised. Five of the six salaried club leaders in Othaya are boys from Wamumu, who have received our training.[12]

Griffin preferred where possible to use ex-Wamumu youths as staff on the clubs' pilot schemes, rather than locally recruited youths. He planned with Captain Gardner to run a three-month training course for 12 or 15 youths at Wamumu, provided that the cost was not to be met by Wamumu. He also drafted the constitution that would govern all youth club operations, and showed how they could cooperate with various youth development programs.

Youth clubs were viewed by the colonial government as having the potential to provide the counterpart among men of the Maendeleo Ya Wanawake (Women's Progress) movement. Because of their success, according to the district commissioner, in his October 4, 1957 communication to the Secretary for Community Development (KNA/CD/36/14/56), the youth clubs in Nyeri were in a rather different position as they had already two schemes well on the way that were being entirely financed by the people in the divisions concerned, Mathira and Othaya, including payment of staff salaries. Provision was made in the 1958 African district council estimates for the payment of some club staff, and a request was made that the Mathira and Othaya schemes be regarded as the pilot schemes for the district. This being the case, it was suggested that funds should be made available immediately to pay for the existing club leaders. To train more of them, money was urgently required, and one or more vacancies were needed at Wamumu for this. Nyeri's district commissioner requested this because more trained leaders were needed to run new schemes. There was strong support for the community development officer's request for a capital grant for the Mathira clubs, and there was an additional request for the funding of six more clubs in Othaya. Although a great deal of money was locally subscribed for the clubs, it was rapidly spent on the payment of the staff rather than on the specific projects that the clubs required. Financial backing by the government during this period was seen as vital with regard to boosting club activities.

Rural and urban youth clubs were developed in association with the JRCs, the state quickly linking the two in an attempt to piece together a coherent strategy that would prevent juvenile migrants from going to Nairobi. The concept of youth clubs had a history stretching back to the late 1930s and 1940s when social programs were developed to occupy African youths in Nairobi. The Boy Scouts, the Young Men's Christian Association, and several events were held in social clubs in African areas infrequently throughout the 1940s.[13] These programs suffered not only from continual funding and personnel shortages, but also from a lack of interest on the part of African youths and administrators. Appropriate utilization of youths' time was a continual concern for officials. Urban migration was often described as the result of boredom in the reserves, and crime in the city was due to a lack of discipline and work. The clubs were expected to develop rural cottage industries and to provide full-time occupational and recreational programs for youth in the hope of stemming the tide of juvenile migration to the cities, especially Nairobi, criminalization, and induction into Mau Mau culture.[14] The youth were to be kept continuously busy with their attention firmly focused away from the bright lights of the city and from taking the oaths of the Mau Mau fighters. The club system was, in many ways, the final component in the expanding "juvenile pipeline." Illustrating this point, Paul Ocobock notes that the Department of Community Development pulled its staff from the adult pipeline and from Wamumu Youth Camp. Screeners and rehabilitation staff involved in community development, such as Peter Moll who had worked at Athi River, were instructed to manage the youth clubs in Nyeri. Within the clubs, some Wamumu graduates were employed as club leaders.[15] They were in charge of discipline and organization and they were paid well for their efforts, earning 150–160 Kenya shillings per month from the African district council coffers or local council authorities. Additional funding for other youth club activities came from charitable organizations such as the Dulverton Trust, government grant-aid programs that were channeled through African district councils or local council authorities to meet material and equipment costs.[16]

The task of the community development officers and youth club leaders was not to rehabilitate suspect Mau Mau members by constructing miniature youth camps across Nyeri but to subvert the Mau Mau's ability to gain new young converts in rural areas. Employing Wamumu youths was not the only connection that the youth clubs had with the expanding juvenile pipeline. In Nyeri, the youth clubs were organized within JRCs. Rural youth club members from the division worked inside, engaging the inmates in physical and intellectual activities to prevent their boredom, escape, and their rejoining the Mau Mau movement. With its connections to the youth club system, the Nyeri JRC developed characteristics beyond that of a "sorting house." John Nottingham observed that a twenty-day program was developed to discourage those who wished to return to the camp. The state used the youth clubs and JRCs together to buttress repatriation and to keep juveniles at home or in their rural homes. The results were effective, with about 55 percent of those brought to the JRC remaining at home.[17]

The primary difference between youth clubs and detention camps was that the clubs were voluntary and lacked many of the punitive elements seen in the JRCs. However, from the research findings, it is evident that some of the training, in which club members were frequently put to work on various infrastructure projects, spilled over into exploitation. For instance, according to the Ministry of Community Development Annual Report, 1959, youth clubs in Kenya as a whole were responsible for the construction of 93 miles of road, 2,438 homes, 31 dams, and 345 miles of enclosure by the end of 1959. In addition, 6,151 acres were harvested and 15,252 acres of land weeded by youth club members.[18] Sports were the centerpiece of most of the community development efforts, and each officer ensured that several tracks and football fields were constructed in the communities. As at Wamumu, sports became a central feature of the Ministry of Community Development's hearts and minds campaign. This enabled the youths to release their energies, show off their prowess and skills, and to create amongst themselves heroes to admire. In general, the clubs kept youths busy, preventing them from engaging in activities that were deemed deviant by the colonial government.

Keen to capitalize on the success of the pilot programs in Nyeri, the government appointed Griffin to be colony youth organizer, to inspect the clubs and to consider how their principles could be applied throughout the rest of Central Province and, later, the entire colony. He was required to make a survey on how the successful the programs of Mathira youth clubs and the character-training center at Wamumu could be combined to address the problem of juvenile delinquency within the colony. In his tour of Central Province, Griffin noted a staggering 200,000 unoccupied youths who could benefit from the clubs. In 1957, the Ministry of Community Development began to spread youth clubs beyond Nyeri with greater assistance from the government. Constant appeals were made to the government for temporary financial assistance to help the clubs survive their first crucial years. By 1958, clubs were in operation in all districts of Central Province, with the exception of Meru, where continued Mau Mau oathing hindered government efforts to start and develop clubs. Further, it was felt by the district community officer for Meru that youth clubs as run and organized in the Kikuyu districts were not the answer for Meru districts, since in Kikuyuland there were large villages and the people were much more densely concentrated; youth clubs were well suited to these regions.

In Meru a large proportion of the youths were either at school or were away herding sheep, cattle, and goats over a wide area.[19]

To address the youth problems in Meru, Thomas Seaward, the district community development officer, embarked on a new scheme which he felt was more practical in the long run and could serve the needs of the district better. This was the apprenticeship training scheme, which was run along the lines of apprenticeships in Britain and also the character training scheme at Gitoro, which was going extremely well and only required broadening with district training courses. In his opinion Seaward only required his staff to be trained for the work as well as 4,000 Kenya shillings to purchase the equipment that was required to start various projects. Most youths wanted the trade training and were especially keen to learn carpentry, because it was much needed in the region. Although Seaward was keen to set up carpentry workshops, he was unable to effect this owing to the lack of funds for vital tools. These funds, according to Griffin, could have been easily provided by the Ministry.[20] Gitoro was seen as a centre of great potential and immense value and it was unfortunate according to Griffin that the character side of the training was disturbed by the youths' discontent over the absence of basic equipment.

It is important to note, however, that later there was a request from the community development officer of Meru to start youth clubs in the district, and there were plans to visit Igembe Division to explore the possibilities there. In addition, there were plans to carry out propaganda meetings to launch the idea and to stir up enthusiasm in the local communities. Further, they made plans to visit Othaya clubs in order to examine their operations and discover how they could be applied in the Meru District. Finally, they earmarked their staff for Wamumu training. Thomas Seaward was the designated leader of the scheme, but John Longhurst was to receive a free hand with regard to clubs' development on the lines that had been agreed by the district commissioner, Thomas Seaward, and Griffin. Three years later, over 150 clubs had been built throughout the colony.[21] They became ideal after-care treatment for the delinquent youths who passed through the JRCs and other elements of the larger rehabilitation process.

It is important to note that during their short existence youth clubs were a means of preventing juvenile migration from the rural areas and provided various activities for idle urban youths. Their later connection with the JRCs was a move to bind first-time offenders and recidivists to the rural areas and break the cycle of rural–urban migration and unemployment. From their inception, the clubs in Nyeri District were extraordinarily successful. They initially attracted from 50 to 100 youths but within a short period, despite their 50 cent tuition fee, each was enrolling between 300 and 500 youths who were eager to take advantage of the skills training and educational courses that they offered.[22] Whether or not the membership was coerced, the bulk of youth club funding came from the local communities. The staff the government provided came from the youths who were trained at Wamumu. Membership to the clubs was confined to those who were under the age of 21. Griffin's views on the need to extend youth clubs to the entire colony were affirmed and strengthened by the work of John Nottingham, a former district officer, who was liberating hundreds of youngsters repatriated from Nairobi in his JRC. This had no barbed wire, and the children who stayed there were not isolated from wider society. Nottingham based his independent attitude on the clear distinction between a wanton criminal attitude and a mere childhood misfortune. He wanted to win the children's confidence, to help with their problems, and to restore their sense of security, while the law required a vagrant to be treated as a criminal.[23] It was with this distinction in mind that Griffin went to Nairobi, and he was disappointed to discover from his observations and from sympathetic district officers such as Elizabeth Jackson at Makadara how in the absence of a constructive rescue program an innocent, wandering child could rapidly turn to genuine crime or unruly behavior.

In his report to the government on the youth problem in Nairobi and the colony as a whole, Griffin was guided by the Geneva Declaration on the Rights of Children, which states that "the child must be the first to receive relief in times of distress, must enjoy full benefits provided by social welfare, social security schemes, must receive the training which can enable him/her at the right moment to earn a livelihood and must be protected from every form of exploitation."[24] The government accepted his report and set up pilot programs in each and every district in Central Province. The community response to youth clubs was overwhelming. They willingly set aside permanent plots for youth clubs, and these were used for learning modern methods of farming and producing food for general consumption. The clubs had a dual role, raising funds and also a psychological strategy for keeping youth busy by engaging them in useful activities. In order to govern their functional processes, Griffin drafted the constitution of the Kenya Association of Youth Clubs, which began functioning in 1958 under its first chair, Sir Godfrey Slade. Griffin became its first secretary and chief executive in 1959, and the Governor of Kenya accepted the presidency of the association. The council comprised the chairperson, the secretary, who also served as the chief executive, the treasurer, and 15 members. The bulk of the supervision work at grassroots level was conducted by government officers in rural districts. In townships, social welfare officers employed by the local councils took responsibility.[25]

The aim of the Kenya Association of Youth Clubs was to develop good citizenship among the youth by teaching them services useful to the public and handicrafts useful to themselves through the provision and fostering of facilities for self-education, healthy recreation, and general good fellowship. It's work was guided by the motto of "Service and High Endeavor." Membership of the association was open to clubs containing young persons between the ages of 13 and 18. In junior clubs, membership was allowed for children between the ages of 7 and 12. The clubs were allowed to cater for any race, sex, or creed. The association was to be void of any connection with a political body, and member clubs were not supposed to take part in political meetings or any other political activities. It was expected that club members should belong to a religious denomination and attend its services. No officer of the association was expected to urge any club member to attend any religious service other than that of the member's own denomination. The association desired friendly relations with other organizations of a nonpolitical nature that had similar aims.[26] The officers of the association comprised of the president, the vice-president, the chairperson, the deputy chairperson, the chief executive officer, the secretary, the treasurer, training officers, supervising officers, and youth club leaders. Complete control of the affairs of the association was vested in the council, which consisted of the following officers of the association: president, vice-president, chairperson, deputy chairperson, chief executive officer, secretary, treasurer, and up to six other members. The chief executive officer and the secretary were nominated by the Minister for Community Development. The chairperson, the deputy chairperson, the treasurer, and six other members were elected at an annual general meeting that was held in Nairobi every quarter. The retiring officers were permitted to offer themselves for reelection during this meeting.[27]

According to the constitution each district supervisory officer and his committee were entitled to cast two votes on behalf of the clubs within that district or township at the annual general meeting. In cases of districts or townships distant from Nairobi, the votes could be cast by Nairobi representatives who were appointed by the district supervisory officer and his committee. Between annual general meetings, the council had the power to coopt such additional members as deemed necessary, and also to fill any vacancies that occurred through the resignation of a member or for any other reason. The council of the association was expected to meet at least once a quarter, and such meetings were expected to be convened by order of the chairperson, the deputy chairperson, the chief executive officer, or by two or more members of the council. Five members of the council were required to form a quorum. Any district association that desired to move any resolution at the annual general meeting was expected to give notice of its intention, in writing to the secretary, at least 30 days prior to the meeting. A provincial supervisory officer for any province could be appointed at any time by a written warrant from the council. His duties were to promote and control the organization and effective working of the association within his province, in conjunction with district supervisory officers within that province. A district supervisory officer was appointed by a written warrant from the council in each district or township where member clubs were formed. His duties were to promote and control the organization and effective working of the association within his district or township, in conjunction with a committee composed of other officers of the association from within that district or township.[28] Youth clubs were expected to be registered with the council of the association, which were to have the power to issue, suspend, or withdraw such registration at its discretion. Applications for registration were to be made through the district supervisory officer, and, where applicable, through the provincial supervisory officer.

Appointments as youth club leaders, salaried or unpaid, were made by a written warrant from the council, which had the power to issue, suspend, or withdraw such warrants at its discretion. Without such a warrant no one could function as an officer of the association. Warrants were normally issued upon the candidate's completion of an approved course of training, but could also be issued directly upon the recommendation of a district supervisory officer. Each member club was required to elect from among its members a chairperson, a deputy chairperson, and a committee. It was the policy of the association that the internal administration and organization of the club be performed by the elected committee under the guidance of a youth club leader. Clubs and club organizations sponsored by other social bodies were allowed to apply for affiliation to the Kenya Association of Youth Clubs if they so desired. The terms and conditions of this were to be decided upon by the council in consultation with the sponsoring body.[29] It was the policy of the association that clubs were to be self-supporting. Permission from the council was required before any club issued a public appeal for funds. Clubs were entitled to require from their members fees, such as entrance fees and subscriptions, that their committees approved. The council was allowed to require that a capitation fee be paid into the general funds of the association. Upon each formation, each club was required to open a savings bank trustee account into which all club moneys were to be paid. The district supervisory officer was to nominate the trustees for all such accounts and was to ensure that an audit was carried out annually. Training courses of any type, designed for either officers or members of the association, was to be laid down and conducted by the chief executive officer, or by such persons as he was to appoint for the purpose. The council at its discretion was to approve badges to be worn by officers, members, or supporters of the association.[30] Entry to youth clubs was mainly through an application by a parent.

One of the greatest problems that confronted Griffin and his team during the early years of the formation of youth clubs was a lack of adequate funds to pay instructors, club leaders, and staff in spite of the generous contributions that came in from local authorities and certain charitable trusts. These funds were only adequate for materials, equipment, and other basic needs. Were it not for the magnificent voluntary service given for so long by so many instructors, the majority of the clubs would have quickly closed down in the early years. Although some clubs closed in the long run, this was seen as a tragedy given the magnificent work that had been done by all those concerned.

Griffin was very grateful for the support he received from the various youth club stakeholders, despite the many financial challenges that were experienced. He noted that despite the enormous challenges that the clubs were experiencing, they were vital in providing opportunities for African youths to access education or training of some type:

> I would like on behalf of our field and community development officers, to express their appreciation of the support they have received from the provincial administration and for the cooperation of the Education, Agricultural, Veterinary and Medical Departments. Similarly, we are very grateful to the Shell and BP Group and the Sheikh Trust for the magnificent contributions they have made to Nairobi clubs. Without this, the progress made during the last year or two would have been impossible. Finally, I do not wish the public to get too rosy a picture of these clubs. They are run on a shoe-string budget, have been set up very largely through a combination of faith, hope and charity, and are to a certain extent a stop-gap in the education system. I expect the clubs to enable many African youths access more education.[31]

In his address to the Kenya Association of Youth Clubs on May 17, 1960, Governor Baring echoed Griffin's sentiments about the vital role that youth clubs were set to play in education and national development. Their role was recognized by the colonial government, which took various steps to attract youths to the clubs. The first of these was to tell them about the importance of the clubs, which was done through chiefs and headmen, but mostly through open-air "*barazas*" (meetings). Unlike Wamumu, youth clubs were home to more formal academic activities, except that students were not allowed to sit for recognized academic examinations and nor were they eligible for transfer to mainstream schools or other educational institutions. Teachers were recruited to handle most of the academic aspects of the clubs, which were registered with the Ministry of Education with Griffin as the manager designate.

In the beginning, charitable contributions towards the financing of training programs at youth clubs and their other expenses came from Kenya Shell and BP, Sheikh Fanzal Hahi Noordin, and Youth Help Campaigns. There were also some overseas donations that covered staff salaries and vital equipment. The latter was made possible by Griffin's Youth Help Campaign tour of the United States in 1962 and later Britain. On the latter trip, he traveled with two SBC youths, George Waigwa and Peter Njenga, to raise funds, publicize the campaign, and create awareness of the poverty, delinquency, and street children situation in Kenya. The trip took nine days. The growing importance of the youth clubs was demonstrated by frequent calls by probation officers and administrators who did not want juveniles to be placed in approved schools, which were viewed as being detached from society. Commenting on the growing demand for youth clubs during this period, Griffin noted that "since we insisted on children in the youth clubs leading normal lives, they gained preference locally and overseas over the more restrictive approved schools."[32]

It is important to note that Griffin's proposal to expand youth clubs across the entire country was viewed with skepticism at first by the Ministry of Community Development and the council of the Association of Youth Clubs. According to Roger Martin, the council was of the opinion that it was not practical to carry out such a program unless special supervisory staff at officer level could be provided, and that at least two officers were required in many districts. It was clear to the council that individual clubs required an adequate staff of paid youth leaders. It was seen as improbable, short of a radical reassessment of priorities, that any substantial sums for salaries, for other recurrent expenses, for capital grants for buildings and equipment, or even to finance club expansion could be found by the government. If local authorities were prepared to meet these expenses, it was unlikely that the government would treat club payments as qualifying for Grant in Aid.[33] The council however, underscored the fact that clubs were likely to make an important contribution to the general wellbeing of their areas and to supply a partial solution to the problem of providing education, occupation, and character training for those youths who were unsuccessful in obtaining places in primary and secondary schools, until such time as they were old enough to seek employment or to work on the land.

By September 1958, the Kenya Association of Youth Clubs had been formed with the motto of "Service and High Endeavor". Two leaders' courses had been completed at Wamumu and participants had been presented with leader's warrants by Askwith, the Commissioner for Community Development, and the Chairman of the Council of the Kenya Association of Youth Clubs. In their training the leaders were reminded of the fact that:

> They were going out to take charge of clubs which had recently been built from funds provided by the people of the area. They were going to help in solving one of the most difficult problems in Kenya and to provide occupation, crafts, and character-training for youths who, as a result of the shortage of schools, were unable to access school or continue their education when they left primary and intermediate school. They were reminded that the parents of the youths were firmly supporting the scheme and this was proved by their generous contributions. The success of the clubs was to depend on their leadership.[34]

By the end of 1958, there were 65 clubs with a total of 10,000 members. Most of these were in rural areas, the majority in the Kikuyu homelands. Among the recruits to the youth clubs were boys and girls who had been arrested and repatriated to their home districts. To publicize the clubs' work further, Askwith requested the association to produce a youth bulletin on the lines of *The African Sports Review*. There were also several requests from the Chairman of the Young Farmers Committee of the Royal Agricultural Society of Kenya and other officials of various Kenya Young Farmers' clubs on whether they could join or their chairperson could be coopted to the council and the association, since some of their goals were similar to those of youth clubs; these clubs were also fading away in Central Province after the State of Emergency.

Griffin also felt that they could be helped in several ways by the Young Farmers' clubs. For instance, there was the possibility of introducing a proficiency badge and certificate for various aspects of farming as in those clubs, together with the information they had about setting up clubs, model farms, uniforms, badges, leaders' handbooks, membership cards, and application forms. Griffin was able to incorporate their expertise on agricultural shows. A union would also provide a great incentive to youth club members on their model farms.

The Catholic Church, through Father Joseph Scarcella, also thought about encouraging the mission to start youth clubs. Griffin was delighted about this move. He made plans to talk with Father Scarcella about cooperation, and provided him with copies of youth club publications. Griffin felt that such cooperation had the potential to make the organization more powerful, providing it with a rapid boost and many collaborative opportunities, as is evidenced in the following letter he wrote to the Commissioner for Community Development on April 25, 1958. He noted:

> Father Joseph Scarcella came to me with many great queries recently and I also gathered that the Catholics are thinking of encouraging their missions to start clubs under our auspices. If this comes about, it will give our organization a very rapid boost. I provided Father Joseph Scarcella with copies of our publications, and he is to visit me next month to talk the matter over in detail. I am fully in favor of our including a Catholic representative on our council. Apart from the foregoing, the fact the C.C.K are represented may give offence unless we include a Catholic also.[35]

He was also in favor of including a Catholic representative on the council; the Christian Council of Kenya (CCK) was already represented.[36]

SALIENT DETAILS THAT WERE ENTAILED IN THE FORMATION OF YOUTH CLUBS

Several details were entailed in the formation of a youth club. They included communities knowing, understanding, and meeting the following criteria:

The Purpose of a Youth Club

Youth clubs were intended to be gathering places for children and young people where they were to be taught the meaning of service, where they were to be encouraged to aspire to higher standards of cleanliness, courtesy, and self-discipline, where they could learn to be literate and to speak English, where they could gain knowledge of better farming methods or useful handicrafts, and where they could enjoy themselves by playing properly organized games and by participating in various recreational activities such as music and drama. According to the Ministry of African Affairs report of 1960, clubs dealt solely with:

> Juveniles who required occupation to prevent them from getting into mischief. The government considered the youth clubs organization to be an integral part of its social services and whose main purpose was a preventative one of providing occupation and recreation for the youth and young persons in the towns and reserves in order to prevent them from drifting into delinquency or actual crime.[37]

Assessing the Demand for a Club

Having defined the particular area where they considered there was a need for a club, the Association of Kenya Youth Clubs was expected to carry out a survey to discover how many of the following were not in school and not fully occupied each day on their parents' land: boys between 13 and 20 years of age; girls between 13 and 20; boys below 13 but over 6; girls below 13 but over 6. They were also expected to check if there were any other youth services in operation (i.e. Boy Scouts) in the area and, if so, how many of the above children belonged to these. Further, they were also required to check how many children in the area failed to matriculate from primary school to intermediate school each year.[38]

Finding Leaders

It was clear that 99 percent of a club's success depended on the quality of its leader. It was useless to start a club, according to the Association of Kenya Youth Clubs, unless there was a good person to run it. The association sometimes helped with training to make a candidate more proficient, but the club was expected to find someone who was prepared to tackle the job, who had the gift of managing young people, and who was enthusiastic about youth work.[39] It had to be someone who was prepared to give up some time each week to instruct club members.

The Club Itself

It was recommended that farming should be included in the training since it provided plenty of work and could also make the club self-supporting in time.

It was always asked if there was a plot of land available centrally so that the farm was not too far from members' villages and homes. Five acres was regarded as a good size of land for farming. To build and equip a club required money. The amount varied greatly according to the area and the type of building, but 300 Kenya shillings was the usual estimate required for starting one. Local people were expected to be able to contribute towards this before the club was established.[40] Another type of club based itself on a welfare or social hall and concentrated on carpentry, blacksmithing, and signwriting, among other courses. A hall had to be available and funds had to be raised for the necessary equipment that was required.

Who to See When Intending to Form a Club

Having collected all this information, the club had to meet the district officer and community development officer, if there were such in the area. They were required to weigh the collected facts and advise whether the project was viable or not. If they were satisfied, they would ask more detailed questions, such as whether a full salary or a nominal monthly sum would be paid to the youth leader from council or other sources.

How the Kenya Association of Youth Clubs Was Expected to Help Youth Clubs

When a new club was formed and the association was satisfied that all was in order, it could then be registered and given coverage under the law pertaining to the formation of societies. After registration, club members could use the official membership cards and badges of the association, and they could participate in the Proficiency Badge Award Scheme. The club could take part in various club competitions and camps that were arranged from time to time. When there was a vacancy, youth leaders were to be considered for training courses. The boys and girls were members of an organization that was expected to eventually have branches all over Kenya.

It is important to note that as the clubs grew, each of them had a boy and girl leader. In most clubs they were full-time workers who were paid 93/50 and 61 Kenya shillings respectively. Some were paid from the African district council funds and some were paid by divisional and community-raised funds. As earlier noted, however, there were many unpaid volunteers, many of whom helped with crafts and literacy.[41] A scheme was arranged whereby a craft instructor could share some of the profits gained through marketing a product. All the youths were encouraged to make full use of the club library, which contained among much else publications on animal and land husbandry, crafts, and allied subjects. All clubs offered literacy courses. For some, this meant the most basic instruction in forming and understanding letters in their own language; in others simple English was taught; and at higher levels there were introductions to simple civics, agricultural theory, and simple arithmetic.[42] Depending on the club leader, some clubs had a code of behavior and leaders dealt sternly with anyone who transgressed it. This attitude was also reflected in the many forms of voluntary service that were undertaken by various clubs. In order to foster the idea of service to the community, leaders set aside one day a week on which all the members would go out to assist someone in need or provide something that was required by the local people, such as constructing a building or a school, or transporting materials required for rebuilding schools. Others undertook to repair houses in their villages.[43]

Within various clubs, a system of proficiency and service badges evolved. These were given to those who had done outstanding work for their community in a voluntary capacity. Each community was required to provide land, buildings, equipment, and the leader's wage from its own resources. The trained leaders were expected to offer sound practical instruction and set a worthy example of loyalty and responsibility in community service. This helped them to gain much respect from parents and community elders. Commenting on the difference the youth clubs were making to societal development, when he was officiating at the opening of one club, Donald Diment, one of the early colonial officials to be involved in the formation of youth clubs, said "I have never seen anything like this ever before in the reserve and the dedication and work of the youth in changing their societies. This is a worthy program that requires all our support."[44] The number one priority for all clubs was all-out support from the government, as the clubs were necessary for societal development. This was expected to be reflected at all administrative levels and not to be dependent on personal enthusiasm. This was expected in turn to make people conscious of the support that they had to give to the clubs. African district councils were expected to be made aware of the importance of having some sort of salaried youth training staff. Employment patterns in the reserves barred genuine youth workers, and until a tradition of youth service appeared, reliance was placed on salaried leaders. Cooperation that could be given by other government departments was expected to be boosted to the full. Their help particularly in land and animal care was seen as invaluable.

It was agreed by the government that youth club activities had to go beyond recreational aspects. Trade and other instruction had to be included to make them more appealing to African youth, who were most anxious to learn something that would bring them money or through which they would be able to gain employment and earn a living. Club leaders were expected to submit a short monthly report and a weekly progress report.[45]

Capital Expenditure in the Building and Running of Clubs

In Central Province, the bulk of the money for the building and running of clubs was raised by donations from local people. Very few difficulties were experienced in the initial days raising in the order of 1,000 Kenya shillings per division, which sufficed for the erection of very good semi-permanent buildings. In many cases plots of land varying between four and fifteen acres were also donated, so that clubs could make themselves self-supporting from the sale of crops in years to come. In the case of Nyeri, the government allocated an initial grant for Central Province of £1,500. This was used to provide badges, publications, and 50 sets of equipment for carpentry, blacksmithing, shoemaking, buildings, signwriting, and tailoring courses.[46] The average membership of a club raised 200 Kenya shillings. Each club member was required to pay an annual subscription of between two and four Kenya shillings, this varying from province to province, and also had to pay tuition fees and uniform fees. Anyone who was unable to pay fees could still be admitted to full membership free of charge, and was also issued a free membership card, a badge, and a uniform. The first subscription was payable on entry. In other provinces clubs were set up in social halls, thus reducing the capital expenditure necessary.[47] There was no government aid and equipment was bought from the money that was given by African district councils, donated by local people, or earned by club members. Clubs such as carpentry paid for themselves in a reasonably short time, because of the various items they were able to make and sell.[48]

Staff Salaries

In Nyeri, government paid 20 youth leaders from Central Province throughout 1958. Salaries varied from £99.12 to £104.50 per annum. African District councils were expected to take over the payment of these salaries in 1959. Nyeri District paid an additional 30 leaders from its own funds, and it was expected that other districts would do the same. There were also a number of leaders who received a token payment of the order of 30 or 40 Kenyan shillings a month from locational or village councils, and there were many who worked in an entirely voluntary capacity. In other provinces other than Central Province, some African district councils used their community development assistants for youth work.[49]

Training and Recurrent Expenditure Within Youth Clubs

Training courses were held at Wamumu, which provided free housing, cooking facilities, and the loan of sports gear among other provisions. Government made an initial grant of £180 that was used to provide food for the 40 Central Province youth leaders during their six week training course. Several African district councils raised the money to send candidates to various courses that were offered at Wamumu. It is vital to note that many individual villages also raised funds to send potential village youth leaders to Wamumu for training. No particular educational qualification was required for leaders to participate in this training. They came from all walks of life. It was envisaged that clubs would easily be able to maintain and improve themselves through membership subscriptions, entrance fees charged to the public for sporting events, plays, and concerts, sales of their farm produce, sales of articles made in their workshops, and from special projects such as building teams that served local communities.[50]

An in-depth examination of the daily routine of youth clubs shows a resemblance to pseudo-academic institutions in terms of their organization and the programs that were offered in them. Although called youth clubs, they had many programs that were similar to those that were offered in regular schools. Commenting on the educational role played by youth clubs during this period, Griffin noted that "we managed to give education, illegal one in the eyes of the Ministry. But at least education of some sort to young boys and girls who otherwise would never have gotten it."[51] The daily routine of activities reflected features of a typical school program. They offered various sports, community service, discipline, and career talks. Sport was very popular, and there were discussions about adding cycling and cricket to the wide range of sport offerings.

Lack of finances was Griffin's major problem in the running of the youth clubs, and it was difficult to retain good teachers because of the minimal pay they were given and the heavy teaching load that was entailed.

Challenges that Youth Clubs Faced

A critical examination of youth participation in the youth clubs indicates that a majority of youths participated because there was something to be gained from the educational courses that were offered. Parents hungry to educate their children were eager to exploit the services of Wamumu-trained youth club leaders. Chiefs, too, pressured youths to attend, as their presence in the reserves posed a threat to authority. Most Africans were not complacent about the standard or scope of education, especially the limited access to it: there was no schooling for most youths after the age of 12, who before they found jobs drifted into undesirable company and habits. However, despite noble expectations from various constituencies, there were several challenges that clubs faced that made their work and sustainability difficult. First, there was limited funding, and even the grant in aid and Dulverton funds that provided salaries were irregular and inadequate.[52] If it had not been for the magnificent voluntary service given for so long by many instructors, most clubs would have closed down much earlier. Secondly, from the onset, the district commissioners were skeptical about the clubs and were not certain about their feasibility, some wanting assurance of some kind about their maintenance and European supervision of their operations throughout their first or two years. Because of these fears, some district commissioners were reluctant to press on with the scheme at full pressure or to devote money from African district councils to the employment of extra staff until such a time as they were completely convinced of the clubs' importance, stability, leadership, and funding, and also the continuity of the Ministry of Community Development's support. Because of these fears, many district commissioners were in favor of smaller clubs instead of large clubs, since they had "less far to fall."[53]

Another challenge that youth clubs faced was that in some areas such as Kisumu and Kericho the clubs did not catch on. Club members lacked initiative, were not responsive to club activities, and expected the leaders to give 100 percent of their time, which was obviously impossible. Additionally, in some clubs such as those in Fort Hall, there was insufficient encouragement of the youth club's own committees and too much direction by the community development advisers and government staff. Most of them lacked the voluntary leadership that was critically needed. Some of them also required persuasion to establish their own "*Ngwatios*" (help your neighbor) groups and to use social halls that were available. In addition, most clubs were for boys alone, few existing for girls. Further, there was a lack of high standards in products and trade training. There were also delays in the opening of clubs in Meru District because of various outbreaks of Mau Mau oathing, even though clubs were seen as preventing the growth of the movement and future war with the colonial state.[54]

Other challenges that youth clubs faced were whether to open small or large clubs, whether to build clubs or to use available halls, or whether to have farms. Griffin was in favor of opening large clubs, because these would enable the Department of Community Development to make best use of their limited facilities in staff and equipment. Affirming his stand on this, in his communication to the Commissioner for Community Development in 1958 Griffin noted:

> Where almost full-time training is to be given, and where we are to attempt ambitious projects such as the teaching of trades, I am afraid that the large club is the only answer. As you know, funds are very limited indeed, and essential equipments cannot be purchased in sufficient bulk to make it possible for large numbers of small clubs to be brought into being. In a similar way, we shall be very short of staff at first, and they will have to be concentrated if they are to do the maximum amount of good. Later, when the position improves, we may be able to fill in with smaller clubs to serve areas where children have far to walk to reach the nearest big one. The size of the club will in no way affect the membership of our new association, and indeed, I anticipate that most clubs in other areas of the colony will be small ones dealing mainly with recreational activities.[55]

In addition, Griffin also favored the building of clubs as opposed to the use of preexisting halls, because it gave members a place of their own for which they could feel affection and proprietary pride. It is important to note, however, that he encouraged various clubs to use social halls in several areas. In 1958, he noted:

> We have, of course been shown by Machakos District that the clubs based on the social hall can achieve good results, and I am quite happy to try the same thing in Fort Hall. I have arranged, therefore, to establish three such clubs in the Kangema Division in addition to the big self-contained club at Gakui, and Nelson Bird will explore the possibilities of later establishing further four more clubs in the Kiharu Division.[56]

He underscored the need to encourage voluntary leadership if the clubs were to succeed, and also at the same time to face the fact that they were going to need many paid leaders. This was based on the experience of *Maendeleo Ya Wanawake*, which had great difficulties in the areas where it had tried to run clubs on a purely voluntary basis. Their difficulties were seen as being inevitably much greater than those of the *Maendeleo Ya Wanawake* since the man was the wage-earner, and was therefore less static and less able to give a great deal of time unpaid as women could do. It was thus prudent, according to Griffin, to encourage African district councils and the locational councils to pay a living wage to as many youth leaders as possible. There were plans too to form club committees to assist in the daily running of the clubs and help to market their products within rural areas. It is important to note that the clubs were expected to be non-political. Further, the provincial commissioner approved the recruitment of ex-Wamumu boys as leaders of various youth clubs. They were required to be members of the division in which they were working.[57]

Another challenge the clubs faced was the issue of teaching or not teaching Africans their local languages. Commenting on this, the Nyeri District Community Development Officer commented:

> The effects of implementing the policy set out therein will cause widespread dissatisfaction amongst the illiterate members of the clubs, who are, of course, those most in need of encouragement and help, if they are to become useful members of the community. I will not comment on the situation which has now been created which put bluntly, is that I can teach a group of Africans to read a "foreign language", but can be sent to prison if I teach them to read and write in their own language. A further difficulty arises that whereas we can find many voluntary teachers prepared to teach literacy in the vernacular, the teaching of English is a specialized subject. I imagine, furthermore, that the degree of supervision, which will be necessary on the part of the community development staff to ensure that no member learns to read his own language while ostensibly being taught to read English, is such that it is impossible to accept.[58]

Nairobi Youth Vagrancy Menace and the Role of Youth Clubs in Addressing the Problem

Owing to the several challenges discussed above, the only youth clubs to remain in consistent, well-funded operation were those in Nairobi—the Starehe and Kariokor youth clubs that were privately run by Griffin with the assistance of Gikubu and Geturo. These two clubs were sponsored by international and local donors, including the Dulverton Trust, Save the

Children Fund, and Sheikh Trust. The clubs' financial difficulties illustrate that parents and youths found little reason to continue their contributions. By the end of the 1950s, youth clubs could be found within the barbed wire fencing of the JRCs. The merger of the two programs indicates that administrators believed vagrants and delinquents rounded up on urban streets could benefit from instruction, and that this would possibly prevent their return to Nairobi. In 1960, the JRCs were handled by the District Commissioner of Nairobi who oversaw the transfer of juveniles from the city to the JRCs and later to the youth clubs. In each of the JRCs, probation officers investigated the youths and made decisions as to their return, while youth club members engaged the inmates in physical and intellectual activities to prevent boredom and escape.[59]

Because of their connection to the youth club system, the JRCs developed characteristics that were beyond a transit camp or a holding center. Commenting on this, Paul Ocobock observes that the state was using the JRCs and youth clubs to buttress repatriation and to force juveniles to stay at home: 55 percent of those brought to the JRCs were returned home and remained there.[60] This, according to the KNA DC/EMB/2/1/1 report by John Nottingham, District Officer, North Tetu, 1959, involved a level of coercion on the part of the state, which put pressure on the parents to pay school or youth club fees, or threatened to prosecute them for underfeeding their children. In addition, the JRCs were also becoming a dumping ground used by chiefs and headmen who found local youths unmanageable. Nottingham was intrigued by the number of African authorities who showed up at the JRCs with their local "ne'er-do-wells." Supporting the above view, Griffin, in his communication to Askwith on June 10, 1958 observed:

> About two thirds of the children in institutional care have parents or relatives in the reserves who would look after them if we could ensure that the children would not decamp again to the towns or get into trouble in the neighborhood. Where one of our clubs is available in the locality, giving the same trade training facilities and chances of recreation as does Wamumu, there is an excellent chance of a boy settling down well.[61]

Ultimately, financial constraints and an African lack of interest severely hampered the preventive potential of the JRCs and youth clubs until the end of the colonial period. Nearly half of the repatriated youths in Nyeri returned to Nairobi after their initial removal. Despite this, the "juvenile pipeline" had not lost its primary function, to act as a conduit for juveniles to be returned home or institutionalized by the state. Because of this, however, the continuing vagrancy within Nairobi was never addressed or adequately solved. Thousands of juveniles were still making their way to the city each year and thousands more were already living there; neither group could find permanent work or education.[62] According to KNA/BZ/5/9 Report on Child Welfare Survey of Problems of Child Welfare in Kenya in 1960, officials warned that vagrant children appeared to constitute the greatest single problem of child welfare in Nairobi, both in terms of numbers and in respect to the moral and physical dangers that beset them. According to the survey, little seemed to have changed in the minds of colonial officials with regard to addressing the increasing levels of child vagrancy in the city. Some still argued that vagrancy was a result of boredom in the reserves, poverty at home, and criminal inclination. The training courses, literacy classes, and labor projects offered in the clubs did not succeed in preventing juveniles from seeking work in Nairobi or turning to subsistence crime when they found none. When the final colonial Vagrancy Act went into effect in 1960, it mentioned juveniles only briefly. Perhaps the colonial state perceived the issue as too complex to manage effectively, or could simply not be bothered with African youths any longer.[63]

Whatever was achieved in the countryside, Nairobi continued to act as a magnet for the dispossessed children of the State of Emergency, and it was no surprise to Griffin when, in August 1958, he was asked by the commissioner to make a tour of the city and work out some proposals for dealing with increasing levels of youth vagrancy there. Several reasons contributed to this. First, there was a breakdown during colonial rule in the moral ties and traditions that were instrumental in fostering customs, respect, and service, which were strong pillars for youth development. These ties were further weakened by the upheaval of the Mau Mau War and the State of Emergency that was declared thereafter. The majority of the youth took to roaming the countryside in gangs. Secondly, schools were not able to provide an answer for the young delinquents for they could not absorb most of them. It was the success of the rural youth clubs that prompted the Department of Community Development to give Griffin the mandate to form youth clubs throughout the country. Describing the gravity of the youth problem in the country by 1962, Griffin observed:

> In February 1962, the Ministry of Education reported a primary school enrolment of 653, 000 children, aged between 7 to 10 years. It was estimated that 119,000 children in this age bracket were out of school. In the

intermediate range between the ages 11 to 14 years, 228,000 children were in school and about 438,000 were not. Of the estimated 600, 000 children between 15 to 18 years, only a small percentage were in secondary school.[64]

The over 200 youth clubs that were formed across the country were all day clubs. They involved about 20,000 young people. In his proposal to the Ministry, Griffin requested the establishment of eight boarding youth clubs in Nairobi, which were to be open all day every day to take care of the increased youth vagrancy in the city. They were expected to provide a full range of training programs. Unlike country youth clubs, the Nairobi ones required boarding provision because the delinquents did not have homes to go back to. Most of the city urchins slept in hideouts and survived by scavenging food from dustbins, bakeries, and food processing backyards. In addition, the heterogeneous city population was not expected to provide support as rural communities had been able to do. Recalling how grave the situation was in Nairobi when he established Starehe and Kariokor youth clubs, Griffin observed:

> I looked around Nairobi and I could see an awful a lot of orphan kids rather like the street boys you see today. They were kids whose fathers had been killed, whose mothers had been forced out of the family land and put into villages and they had run away looking for something to do. Looking in particular if they could find education. And I looked at these kids on the streets and I took an interest in them. So, I went to my Ministry and I said, look, why don't we start a residential youth club here in Nairobi to care for them.[65]

The ministry was opposed to Griffin's suggestions, since it did not want to support anything that would attract attention to the failures of the colonial administration with regard to youth care. In addition, by this time independence was beginning to loom and the colonial government was not interested in starting new initiatives. From the start there was no money from the government to fund Nairobi clubs, which forced Griffin to approach the Sheikh Trust and Shell and BP for help. With land and buildings loaned by the provincial administration and the active help of former staff and boys from Wamumu, the Kariokor and Starehe youth clubs were born. It was during this period that Griffin wrote a letter to Gikubu and Geoffrey Geturo requesting them to join him in the running of these new clubs. At the time Gikubu was working at Othaya Approved School in

Nyeri with Roger Owles, while Geturo was working with Gailey and Roberts in Nairobi. Gikubu did not respond to Griffin's invitation until two months later, after Griffin had written a second letter. He discussed the matter with Owles and without much hesitation left Othaya for Nairobi. He did not know what the future held for him in terms of job salary and security. Commenting on his conviction that he should be part of Griffin's dream, Gikubu remarked: "I left my employment without a second thought. But I was hopeful, trusting, and determined that we could make a difference in the lives of the youth by offering them a rich education."[66]

A closer examination of the work of youth clubs illustrates that they were by no means a progressive advancement in social services on the part of the colonial regime. On one hand, they were a colonial reaction to socio-economic forces that the State of Emergency policies had unleashed and on the other hand they were an attempt to occupy the time and minds of the poor and uneducated rural youths, and to keep their migratory feet firmly grounded in rural reserves. Moreover, the ad hoc nature of the early State of Emergency gave way to community development, and the provincial administration linked youth clubs to the preexisting juvenile pipeline. Officials believed that they had finally developed a system that would cleanse the young people of their Mau Mau oaths, accurately sort them, and transport them to appropriate institutions or back to their homes, thereby preventing the future spread of the Mau Mau movement.[67] However, signs of strain were beginning to materialize under the weight of the sheer numbers of juveniles caught up in the pipeline and the government's quickly dwindling coffers. Yet rather than dismantle the pipeline, the state sought to preserve its new-found relationship with the youths as far as possible. Given the acknowledgments that the youth clubs were receiving locally from parents who were seeking additional admission places for their children and external requests from other African nations to adopt the Kenyan model in addressing similar problems in their own countries, it can be argued that the youth clubs in their short period of existence were a success, despite the challenges they faced.

The youth clubs had a solid two-year run before experiencing a rapid decline. Funding quickly dried up as less and less money could be extracted from local communities. Describing the tight financial budget situation in which the youth clubs operated during this period, Griffin noted in his 1960 report during the general meeting for the Kenya Association of Youth Clubs that "the clubs are run on a shoe-string budget and have been set up very largely through a combination of faith, hope, and charity and are to a certain extent a stop gap in the educational system, which I think will continue for a very long time."[68] In addition, the treasury was not willing to permit the government to provide staff and funds to the youth scheme without a similar contribution by African district councils. It was probable, therefore, that African district councils were required to employ all staff in connection with the scheme but were expected to claim from the government 45 percent of other recurrent expenditures. Although they had a short existence, Griffin noted that "although simple in their programs, they provided an education of some sort to the youth who lacked access to education at the time."[69]

Offering of Literacy in Youth Clubs

It is important to note that although youth club programs were supplementary to the mainstream educational programs, they were of low quality and were constantly faced with lack of funds, trained personnel, and vital equipment. This was because, as earlier observed, they were mainly community-funded projects that received minimal help from the government. In addition, the students who attended youth clubs were not allowed to sit for recognized academic examinations, nor were they permitted to transfer to mainstream schools at a later stage. The question of literacy and whether it should be offered within youth clubs was never adequately addressed by the Ministry of Education. There were constant debates about this, and the required safeguards and conditions that could govern the subject's provision without turning clubs into illegal schools. The government's policy reversals and the debates that took place between the Ministry of Education and provincial and district education officers is a subject that deserves discussion, as evidenced in the following communication from Griffin to the Permanent Secretary for Community Development, dated September 5, 1957. Griffin sought clarification on the way forward. He wrote:

> The importance of offering literacy in youth clubs cannot be over-estimated. I would request that the Education Department be approached for a ruling on the matter. Provided that it is made clear that we aim at literacy in the vernacular tongues, and in English only, I cannot see what valid objection can be raised. Any policy of forcing children to remain illiterate is defensible. As a matter of practical politics, offering literacy will be a major inducement in attracting youths to the clubs.[70]

OFFERING OF LITERACY IN YOUTH CLUBS   109

Discussing the question further, Francis Loyd, Provincial Commissioner, Central Province, wrote to the Secretary for Community Development, Nairobi, on October 22, 1957, and gave several conditions regarding the teaching of literacy in youth clubs:

> The District Officers and District Education Officers should be informed in advance of when and where classes are held and they should participate in the screening of instructors. A list of all instructors should be kept in the education office. Registration and approval of classes should be held at the district and provincial levels. There should be two registers at the district level, one for classes and one for teachers, giving a complete record of the process.[71]

This was regarded as a relatively simple procedure, and the only point that required clarification was whether the scheme as a whole was supposed to be registered with the district community development officer as a manager, or whether each district was required to make its own arrangements with the District Education Board. Several further debates ensued. The debates underscored the colonial education policy principle: that Africans should not be offered even the most basic forms of education. It is important to note that despite the spirited debates against the offering of literacy in youth clubs, the Ministry of Education finally agreed that it was important to offer it. Literacy levels varied across various youth clubs. Some youths were illiterate, others had a rudimentary knowledge, and some had attained a Grade 4 or higher level of education. To cater for various literacy levels, it was proposed that each one should be taught by a club member who was capable of doing so. Instructors for literacy classes were expected to give their services for free and were to receive instructional materials and training from their locational supervisors. The subjects to be taught in literacy classes included reading and writing in Kikuyu and English. No Kiswahili or instruction in other subjects was to be included. There were, however, lectures to be given on health, hygiene, agriculture, law and order, and other non-scholastic subjects.[72] No member of literacy classes was to be under the age of 13, with ages ranging from 14 to 21. In order to maintain supervision and efficiency, classes were to be held once a week. They were to be supervised by the Community Development Officer. It was understood that literacy classes were not to be developed as in schools: they were intended purely as a measure to keep young people out of mischief and at the same time to develop their character. There is no doubt that the inclusion of literacy in youth clubs greatly increased the membership of clubs and decreased juvenile delinquency within Nyeri District.[73] To expedite literacy classes, Mathira literacy project was begun as a pilot scheme for the rest of the district, and later for the colony.

Stringent colonial government regulations and a lack of clarity around the subject hampered many of the students who attended youth clubs from pursuing academic subjects beyond what they were getting from the clubs, despite this having been one of the main factors that had attracted them to join the clubs in the first place, and had encouraged most communities in the case of Nyeri District to donate their meager resources to the process. In addition, some African politicians were suspicious of the activities of the youth clubs. They viewed young Africans who were forced into intensive work without pay as conscripted labor.[74] On the other hand, owing to the educational activities, there were some Africans who praised youth club programs. They saw them as providing an opportunity for the youth to access education and literacy.

Although notions of African youth were clearly changing, the youth clubs had a short life span owing to the high level of costs that were entailed. During this period, local funds and attendance dwindled. The only youth clubs that remained in consistent, well-funded operation as earlier mentioned were those in Nairobi, which were sponsored by international donors. By 1960, Griffin, in his annual report to the Ministry of Community Development, estimated that there were 95 operational youth clubs in Kenya with over 11,071 juveniles in attendance. It is essential to note that youth clubs were not abandoned by the colonial state at the end of the State of Emergency, nor were they closed in the postcolonial period (Figs. 4.1, 4.2, and 4.3).[75]

Despite the enormous challenges that most youth clubs faced during this period, Starehe and Kariokor youth clubs in Nairobi succeeded very well because of Gikubu's devotion to the work. Without his support it would have been difficult for Griffin's work to succeed. Gikubu believed in Griffin and gave generously of his time and service. He was an efficient administrator in youth educational matters having gained enormous experience at Manyani and Wamumu. He worked closely with a team of spirited expatriates that served SBC for many years and established strong cooperative relations with Griffin. It was this team that enabled Gikubu to further his educational work among the youth, especially at SBC. Through their work, more than 12,000 boys from deprived conditions were able to receive a sound education. Gikubu's 55 years' devotion to Kariokor youth club and later SBC, when Kariokor and Starehe youth clubs were merged,

Fig. 4.1 Kariokor youth club (Photo by author from Starehe School archives)

Fig. 4.2 Starehe youth club (Photo by author from Starehe School archives)

demonstrates that indeed he was called upon to educate youth. Affirming this, and summing up Gikubu's enormous role in the growth of the two clubs and later the SBC, Griffin wrote:

> Here and there, of course, one does find administrators who have settled to a lifetime of service, at Starehe, we have some like Gikubu who have been with us for over thirty years. He is one of the pillars of this school and indeed Kenyan youth education. We began with him when Starehe and Kariokor were just mere youth clubs and he was just in his early twenties then. Over the years, observing Gikubu's devotion to youth education, it has been clear to me that indeed he was called to educate the youth and to serve the less fortunate in society. He is a truly Kenyan hero in the field of youth education.[76]

OFFERING OF LITERACY IN YOUTH CLUBS 113

Fig. 4.3 Boys who joined Starehe and Kariokor youth clubs at an early stage (Photo by author from Starehe School archives)

The activities of Starehe and Kariokor youth clubs further steered Gikubu's involvement in Kenyan youth education. His activities as a youth trainer in Starehe and Kariokor youth clubs indicate his continuous quest to provide education and to do something more for young people. As a youth trainer, his work involved going to the streets, alleys, and youth hideouts and convincing them to join Starehe and Kariokor youth clubs in order to gain better housing, food, clothing, and education. He was instrumental in organizing all the youth activities at the clubs that involved admission, character training, and grouping them into various training activities, using the limited resources that were available. He also supervised the training in various trades. Additionally, he was in charge of the recreational and sporting activities that were offered every evening. Further, Gikubu was in charge of all the boarding and dining activities. He ensured the youths were safe at night and helped the security team guard the two clubs' meagre resources. He also worked closely with probation officers, caseworkers, the police, and courts to ensure that cases relating to youths admitted to the clubs were properly handled and the necessary paperwork completed. Speaking of Gikubu's enormous work at the two clubs and contributions to youth education during this period, Griffin opined:

> Gikubu was our stronghold in our work at Kariokor and Starehe youth clubs. I have no words to describe the incredible work he did during this period. He was full of energy and he worked around the clock, 24 hours a day, seven days a week. He was with me during the day searching for the street urchins, brought them to Starehe and Kariokor youth clubs, he ensured they had taken a shower, eaten, were clothed and had a place to sleep. The next day, he was with me again ensuring they were disciplined, were given training and in the evening he ensured they were participating in sports. He worked closely with probation officers, caseworkers, the courts, and the police to ensure that the youths paper work was completed. The story of youth clubs, Starehe, and the Kenyan youth education cannot be written without mentioning his contributions to the process.[77]

This chapter underscores in detail the general functions of the youth clubs and the early roles they played in laying the foundation for Kenya's primary and secondary education in the post-colonial period. It is this role that is significant especially when we examine the work of SBC during this period and Gikubu's educational work in this regard, as Chap. 5 will demonstrate. This chapter illustrates in depth the minimal educational opportunities that existed for Africans in the colonial period, the enormous effects of this on the youth, and how the situation was worsened with Kenya's independence struggle and the waste of lives that accompanied the process. It was in this educational quagmire that the youth clubs were formed. Here much of Gikubu's experience in Kenyan youth education was developed, later being enhanced at SBC after the merger of Kariokor and Starehe youth clubs. It was from these educational ashes that SBC rose and Gikubu's full engagement in Kenyan youth education work enhanced.

Notes

1. Paul Ocobock, "Joy Rides for Juveniles: Vagrant Youth and Colonial Control in Nairobi, Kenya, 1901–1952," *Social History,* 31.1 (2006): 39–59.
2. Geoffrey Griffin, *School Mastery: Straight Talk about Boarding School Management* (Nairobi: Lectern Publications, 1996), 46.
3. Yusuf King'ala, *The Autobiography of Geoffrey William Griffin: Kenya's Champion Beggar* (Nairobi: Falcon Crest, 2005).

4. King'ala, *The Autobiography of Geoffrey William Griffin: Kenya's Champion Beggar*.
5. Beecher Report on African Education in Kenya, 1949, p. 34.
6. Ocobock, "Joy Rides for Juveniles: Vagrant Youth and Colonial Control in Nairobi, Kenya, 1901–1952".
7. Ibid.
8. Ibid., 59.
9. Peter Moll's summary of the main objectives, aims, and activities of the youth clubs in Mathira Division, Nyeri District by August 1956 when they were formed.
10. Ocobock, "Joy Rides for Juveniles: Vagrant Youth and Colonial Control in Nairobi, Kenya, 1901–1952".
11. Documentary Interview, Geoffrey Griffin, September 4, 2004.
12. Geoffrey Griffin's communication KNA/CYC/POL/8 to the District Community Development Officer, Nyeri District on his preference to use Othaya youth clubs instead of Mathira youth clubs as pilot schemes since he had trained most of their leaders at Wamumu.
13. Peter Ojiambo, *Teaching Beyond Teaching: Geoffrey William Griffin and Starehe Boys Centre and School* (Saarbrucken, Germany: VDM Verlag, 2008).
14. Ibid.
15. Ibid.
16. Ibid.
17. John Nottingham's report KNA DC/EMB/2/1/1 on how the colonial government used youth clubs and Juvenile Reception Centres to buttress repatriation and to keep juveniles at home or in their rural homes.
18. Work done by youth clubs according to the Ministry of Community Development Annual Report, 1959.
19. Yusuf King'ala, *The Autobiography of Geoffrey William Griffin: Kenya's Champion Beggar*.
20. Ibid.
21. Ibid.
22. Ocobock, "Joy Rides for Juveniles: Vagrant Youth and Colonial Control in Nairobi, Kenya, 1901–1952".
23. King'ala, *The Autobiography of Geoffrey William Griffin: Kenya's Champion Beggar*.
24. Geneva Declaration on the Rights of Children, 1948.
25. Kenya Association of Youth Clubs manual, 1958.
26. The constitution of Kenya Association of Youth Clubs, 1958.
27. Ibid.
28. Ibid.
29. Ibid.

30. Ibid.
31. Ibid., 64.
32. Ibid., 57.
33. Roger Martin, *Anthem of Bugles: The Story of Starehe Boys Centre and School* (Nairobi: Heinemann Educational Books Ltd., 1978).
34. Leaders training at Wamumu and the emphasis of the courses that were offered as provided in KNA/Y/40/2/1 report by Askwith, the Commissioner for Community Development and the Chairman of the Council of the Kenya Association of Youth Clubs dated February 26, 1958.
35. Geoffrey Griffin's communication to the Commissioner for Community Development KNA/CYC/COL/GEN/30 dated April 25, 1958 explaining the need to incorporate various organizations and individuals in the work of youth clubs for instance, churches (i.e. Catholics and other churches under the auspices of the Council of Christian Churches of Kenya).
36. Okwach Abagi and Ibrahim Ogachi, *Fifty Years of Education Development in Kenya: Mapping Out the Gains, Challenges and Prospects for the Future* (Nairobi: The Jomo Kenyatta Foundation, 2014).
37. The Ministry of African Affairs report of 1960, KNA/ DC/GRSSA/7/22 outlining the main objectives of youth clubs.
38. Kenya Association of Youth Clubs manual, 1958.
39. Ibid.
40. Ibid.
41. The constitution of Kenya Association of Youth Clubs, 1958.
42. Documentary Interview, Geoffrey Griffin, September 4, 2004.
43. Ibid.
44. Donald Diment, one of the early colonial officials who was heavily involved in youth club formation, commented KNA/NY/3/1 on the difference the youth clubs were making to societal development when officiating over the opening of one of the youth clubs to be formed, on June 3, 1958.
45. Documentary Interview, Geoffrey Griffin, September 4, 2004.
46. Ibid.
47. The constitution of Kenya Association of Youth Clubs, 1958.
48. Documentary Interview, Geoffrey Griffin, September 4, 2004.
49. Ibid.
50. Ibid.
51. King'ala, *The Autobiography of Geoffrey William Griffin: Kenya's Champion Beggar*, 69.
52. Ibid.
53. Documentary Interview, Geoffrey Griffin, September 4, 2004.
54. Roger Martin, *Anthem of Bugles: The Story of Starehe Boys Centre and School*.
55. Geoffrey Griffin's communication to the Commissioner for Community Development KNA/CYC/CP/GEN/53 in 1958 on his views on the

need to open large clubs as opposed to small clubs. The large clubs would according to him have enabled the department to make best use of their limited facilities and staff.
56. A communication KNA/ CYC/CP/GEN/FH/16/58 from Geoffrey Griffin to the District Commissioners illustrating his preference for building clubs as opposed to using social halls to house them. He argued that the former provided members with a place of their own for which they could feel affection and a proprietary pride. However, he encouraged various clubs to use social halls in situations where they were unable to build their own.
57. Peter Ojiambo, *Teaching Beyond Teaching: Geoffrey William Griffin and Starehe Boys Centre and School* (Saarbrucken, Germany: VDM Verlag, 2008).
58. A communication KNA/CD/NY/3/1 from the District Community Development Officer, Nyeri dated September 19, 1957 arguing for the need to teach African youths their local languages.
59. Ojiambo, *Teaching Beyond Teaching: Geoffrey William Griffin and Starehe Boys Centre and School*.
60. Ibid.
61. A communication KNA/CYC/KAYC/ORG/49 from Geoffrey Griffin to Askwith dated June 10, 1958 illustrating how the Juvenile Reception Centers were being used by various African authorities as dumping grounds for unmanageable youths.
62. Roger Martin, *Anthem of Bugles: The Story of Starehe Boys Centre and School*.
63. Ocobock, "Joy Rides for Juveniles: Vagrant Youth and Colonial Control in Nairobi, Kenya, 1901–1952."
64. King'ala, *The Autobiography of Geoffrey William Griffin: Kenya's Champion Beggar*, 58.
65. Television Interview, Geoffrey Griffin, May 6, 2000.
66. Interview, Joseph Gikubu, August 27, 2013.
67. Ojiambo, *Teaching Beyond Teaching: Geoffrey William Griffin and Starehe Boys Centre and School*.
68. Geoffrey Griffin's report KNA/MCD/10/1/8 during the general meeting for the Kenya Association of Youth Clubs in 1960, describing the tight financial budget situation in which the youth clubs operated.
69. Television Interview, Geoffrey Griffin, May 6, 2000.
70. Geoffrey Griffin's communication KNA/CYO/POL/5 to the Permanent Secretary for Community Development dated September 5, 1957, seeking clarification on the way forward with regard to the offering of literacy classes within youth clubs.
71. Francis Loyd, the Provincial Commissioner, Central Province letter to the Secretary for Community Development, Nairobi, KNA/PRIS/25/6/1/70

dated October 22, 1957, giving several conditions that were required for the teaching of literacy in youth clubs.
72. Documentary Interview, Geoffrey Griffin, September 4, 2004.
73. Ibid.
74. Ojiambo, *Teaching Beyond Teaching: Geoffrey William Griffin and Starehe Boys Centre and School.*
75. Television Interview, Geoffrey Griffin, May 6, 2000.
76. Geoffrey Griffin, *School Mastery: Straight Talk about Boarding School Management*, 46.
77. Ibid., 48.

CHAPTER 5

A Flower in the Mud: The Founding of Starehe Boys Centre and School and Its Growth

Whatever else Gikubu may have accomplished during his involvement in Kenyan youth education, his cofounding and development of Starehe Boys Centre and School (SBC) will forever remain his lasting contribution. The founding of SBC in 1959 is embedded in Kenya's educational historical context in both the colonial and postcolonial periods. In the colonial period, SBC depicts the nature of colonial education, which was racial, segregative, and inadequate, and whose policies locked most Kenyan youths out of the education system. It was this lack of access to education that led to an increase in youth vagrancy, which the formation of youth clubs, as discussed in Chap. 4, helped to alleviate. The postcolonial period shows SBC's transition from a youth club to a center and eventually to a school, from 1963 to the present, and its contributions to the development of modern Kenyan secondary education. The educational programs that were undertaken by SBC in both periods and the difficulties encountered reflect the wider Kenyan and African educational efforts that were made in both periods to address societal needs. In order to comprehend the role of Gikubu in the Kenyan youth education through his work at SBC it is vital to examine the larger historical context in both periods.

SBC's Educational Work in the Colonial Period

The founding of SBC, which begun with its formation as a youth club, is embedded in Kenya's political, historical, social, cultural, and economic contexts. It took place at a time when Kenya was struggling for independence, a period marked by the Mau Mau War against the British colonial government. Some of the youths admitted to the new club had certainly fallen foul of the law, but through no fault of their own. Seven years earlier, before the formation of SBC, in October 1952, the nationalist movement in Kenya had shown its hand with the killing of Senior Chief Waruhiu, well known for his loyalty to the colonial government. A few days later, Governor Evelyn Baring declared a State of Emergency, setting the stage for the final, conclusive struggle that was to lead to Kenya's independence. During the Mau Mau War, thousands of men, most of them heads of families, were arrested and held in detention camps; others lost their lives through their refusal to support the nationalist cause. In the Kikuyu reserves, countless families lost their identity when forced to move into temporary fortified villages. Traditional customs and loyalties, sorely beset since the coming of the colonial rule, disintegrated still further under the intolerable pressures of the time; and more and more children, especially boys, found themselves without the support of parents and family. There was no refuge in the country for these homeless youths. With no prospects and little or no support from the state, even the youngest were caught up in the inevitable trek to Nairobi, that distant, glamorous city whose streets were paved with gold. Hundreds of them took to roaming the streets, begging and mugging, and youth vagrancy increased. The foundation of Starehe was a response to the colonial state's inability to eradicate the problem of juvenile delinquency and to address overall access to education for African youth. Summing up the historical events that led to the founding of SBC and the state of youth education during this time, Kennedy Hongo and Jesse Mugambi write:

> Loitering on the streets of Nairobi were many helpless children especially boys left as orphans due to the deaths of their fathers during the Mau Mau struggle or as a result of the imprisonment of their fathers in detention camps. These youths wore tattered clothes, had barefoot and had nowhere to sleep. They had no food to eat and indeed looked very dirty, helpless, and sickly. For their daily survival, they ate left-overs thrown into dustbins and the older ones had to pick pocket in order to find money to buy food. They slept by the riverbanks and in some city corridors in the cold. Most of them were not

going to school and even if they wanted they were few schools that could absorb them.¹

During this period, there was a significant increase in the number of destitute children and juvenile delinquency in Nairobi, larger than in any other town in Kenya. Police figures from this period record thousands of vagrant children, a high number compared with Nairobi's relatively small population. Roger Martin observes that the educational possibilities for a destitute child in the city were abysmal in 1959. Out of 15,000 children of primary school age, there were 10,000 not in school at all, with many others only in school on a part-time basis owing to overcrowding. About 300 children left school each year after Standard Four, and many of them were below the employment age of 16.² The conditions of the time led to increased levels of vagrant activities partly because of a lack of parental control and partly because youths were forced to use any means necessary to survive. Exploring the state of youth vagrancy during this period, Griffin gives the following figures to illustrate its magnitude and how it was accelerated because of limited schooling for Africans:

> In February 1962, the Ministry of Education reported a primary school enrolment of 653,000 children aged between 7 to 10 years. It was estimated that 119,000 children in this age bracket were out of school. In the intermediate level between the ages 11 to 14 years, 228,000 children were in school and about 438,000 were not! Of the estimated 600,000 children between 15 to 18 years, only a small percentage were in secondary schools!³

The situation was worsened further during the Mau Mau war and after the declaration of the State of Emergency by the colonial government. During this period, there was a rapid increase in juvenile delinquency and youth vagrancy, and the methods that were used by the colonial government, such as the use of juvenile courts, approved schools, and repatriation orders, could not alleviate the problem. According to Griffin "it was a grotesque exercise. They would ask where a boy came from. He would give them a wrong address and they'd just take him out on a lorry and drop him in the country side. The kid would walk straight back to Nairobi."⁴

It was under these conditions that Griffin was appointed as a youth colony organizer by the colonial government in late 1957 and transferred to Nairobi. His mandate included establishing youth clubs throughout the country and training youth leaders to run them. The purpose of the clubs, as discussed in Chap. 4, was to aid national development by supplementing the work of schools and absorbing some of the footloose youths who had grown up during the State of Emergency period and were engaging in all kinds of vagrant activities, such as petty theft, vandalism, and violence. Griffin took on his new role with determination. By September 1958 the Kenya Association of Youth Clubs had been formed, with Griffin's striking motto of "Service and High Endeavour," two leaders' courses had been completed at Wamumu, and there were already 65 clubs with a total of 10,000 members. The clubs, which were self supporting, were mostly in rural areas, the majority in Kikuyu homelands. The recruits included both boys and girls who had been arrested in Nairobi and forcibly repatriated to their home districts. But whatever was achieved in the countryside, the city continued to act as a magnet for dispossessed children. Until Starehe and Kariokor youth clubs opened their doors, there was almost no attempt made by the colonial government to care for the hordes of children living on the streets of Nairobi. Commenting on the deplorable conditions for youth in this period and the lack of adequate colonial approaches to address their plight, Roger Martin states:

> A church club at Karen met once a week, another in Pumwani on two evenings. The Christian Industrial Training Centre in Pumwani offered a full-time training course, but only for those who had reached standard seven in primary school, and furthermore on a fee-paying basis. The excellent Save the Children Fund Home for the helpless children at Ujana Park had closed early in 1958. There was virtually nothing else. All that a boy could look forward to was a periodic arrest, judicial beatings, and perhaps "repatriation" to his home area, where he would be unwelcome and from which he would promptly return to Nairobi, and eventually, an approved school. The city authorities showed little enthusiasm for clubs, such well-meaning ventures could only serve to attract still more youngsters to the capital, and their sole desire was to clear the streets.[5]

It was thus no surprise to Griffin when, in August 1958, he was asked to take a tour of Nairobi and work out some proposals for dealing with vagrancy in the city. His views were strengthened and clarified by his friendship with John Nottingham, the North Tetu District Officer who had been removed from detention camp administration and was now devoting himself to the liberation of the hundreds of youngsters who had been repatriated from Nairobi to his Juvenile Reception Centre (JRC). This did not have barbed wire surrounding it, and the children who stayed there were not isolated from the rest of society: they were allowed to mix with the community. Nottingham based his independent attitude on the clear distinction between wanton crime and mere childhood misfortune. He wanted to win the children's confidence, to help them deal with their problems, and to restore their sense of security against the demands of the law, which required a vagrant child to be treated as a criminal. It was with this distinction in mind that Griffin went to Nairobi, and he was unconvinced that, even in the absence of a constructive rescue program and structures that addressed the problem, an innocent wandering child would rapidly turn to genuine crime, basing this view on his own observations and the reports of sympathetic district officers such as Elizabeth Jackson who was in charge of Makadara.

In his report, he requested the formation of at least eight clubs in the city, which would have to be open all day every day and provide a full range of training programs. Among the possible sites he noted was "a community centre, built in stone with an adjacent playing field, at Starehe."[6] He thought that the colonial government would take the lead in financing the venture, since the heterogeneous city population could not be expected to support it in the same way that rural communities were able to support similar schemes. Griffin's proposal was rejected by the city authorities and the central colonial government. Since independence was nearing they did not want to attract attention to anything that could be seen as the failure of the government in tackling youth vagrancy. Building such a centre would have caused enormous pressure and bad publicity, attracting the international community's attention to the plight of children in the colony and adding fuel to the independence movement. It was at this point that Griffin got fed up, approached the permanent secretary to whom he reported, and asked if he could start a private youth club. According to Yusuf King'ala, he received a classic civil service reply: "as long as you don't ask for money and as long as this work does not interfere with your proper duties, I don't mind what you do."[7] It was with this assurance that Griffin set off to start Kariokor and Starehe youth clubs.

Although the colonial government and the city council declined to finance the clubs in any way, Griffin persuaded the provincial administrator, Richard Wilkinson, to identify sites and buildings. Wilkinson granted him the use of Kariokor and Starehe community halls. Summing up how he began SBC and the forces that guided its founding, Griffin noted:

> I noticed many ragged children on the streets of Nairobi. Obviously underfed, stealing everything they would lay their hands on and heading for a life of total crime and it was time somebody got in and did something. So, I went to the government and said, look you know we've got to do something about these kids. So they said okay. What do you want to do? You want to start more approved schools? And I said, for God's sake no! I had no higher opinion of approved schools. Wamumu was the answer. Because that worked. I thought we would probably introduce this into some sort of youth centres. And that spread like wild fire all over the country. That is how Starehe and Kariokor youth clubs begun.[8]

More help came from private sources. Although Griffin was uncertain about where to find funds to run his newly formed clubs, he had faith that somehow he would get some help—relying on God to start the process. He observed that "faith in those days was some kind of capital."[9] Narrating his miraculous encounter with Shell/BP, which eventually became an SBC key donor, Griffin recalled:

> As I walked down the present day Harambee Avenue, I stopped near a building and walked in. I asked the receptionist if they had a Public Relations Officer. It turned out to be Shell/BP and I was led to its Public Relations Officer, Mr. John Francis. I explained to him my mission of trying to rescue Mau Mau orphans from the streets of Nairobi. I managed to interest him and took him in my car to show him the hideouts of the street waifs. On the tour, he was able to see the terrible conditions under which the poor boys lived, collecting bread leftovers and fruit peel from dustbins. He became convinced as me that something needed to be done. He was touched and decided to support me.[10]

This marked the beginning of the funding partnership between SBC and Shell/BP, which has remained to date. Shell/BP made the initial grant of £2000. In addition to this financial help, the company also granted SBC two tin huts, which served as dormitories and later classrooms for the first 17 boys who joined the school. On November 14, 1959, Starehe Youth Club was officially opened. The occasion was graced with the attendance of various distinguished guests, including the Minister for African Affairs, Charles Johnson. As time passed more funds and offers came in from private sources; for instance, the Sheikh Fazal Ilahi Noordin Charitable Trust, the Child Welfare Society, the Kenya Welfare Trust, and the African Welfare Trust. Several local firms supplied building materials and advice.

Fig. 5.1 Two tin huts where Starehe Boys Centre and School begun (Photo by author from Starehe School archives)

Additionally, fruitful contacts were made with juvenile courts, the Minister for African Affairs, and Dorothy Hughes, the doyenne of welfare work in Kenya and a former member of the Legislative Council. Other support in the initial stages came from Youth Help Campaigns through the Child Welfare Society. To boost support for the Youth Help Campaigns, Griffin traveled to London with two boys, George Waigwa and Peter Njenga, with the aim of raising "funds and creating awareness of poverty, youth delinquency and the need for help in order to arrest the situation."[11] Further support came from Thomas Mboya, the area Member of Parliament, who was the first African political leader to become interested in SBC's work (Figs. 5.1, 5.2, and 5.3).

After obtaining land and initial financial help, Griffin searched for people who could help him with the work. He needed people who understood what he was doing, and it was at this time that he requested Joseph Gikubu and Geoffrey Geturo to join him. The two men, together with Griffin, became cofounders of SBC. Both were in gainful employment at this time: Gikubu was working at Othaya Approved School in Nyeri while Geturo was working with Gailey and Roberts in Nairobi. Both had

Fig. 5.2 Geoffrey Griffin and two boys, Peter Njenga and George Waigwa of Starehe Boys Centre and School in London 1962, as part of youth help campaign to raise funds for the school (Photo by author from Starehe School archives)

promising careers but were determined to work with Griffin even if their salaries and the longterm funding of the school were uncertain. Gikubu was appointed to Starehe on June 30, 1959. This was the beginning of his engagement in Kenyan youth education, which would last 55 years. Given his busy work as a youth colony organizer, Griffin realized it was going to be difficult for him to manage the daily running of the two clubs. To ease the administration, he put Gikubu in charge of the Kariokor Youth Club and Geturo in charge of the Starehe youth club (Figs. 5.4 and 5.5).

It is important to note that the initial plans for starting numerous clubs in Nairobi did not materialize. A third club at Doonholm Road, Makadara, specializing in tailoring, closed early in 1962 owing to poor levels of supervision and instruction. Even before this, in August 1961, Griffin had already decided to absorb the Kariokor youth club into the more spacious grounds at Starehe, believing that centralization was the best option for effective management. He asked Gikubu to move to Starehe, to work under Geturo. In September that year, the first 50 youths were transferred from

Fig. 5.3 Geoffrey Griffin and two boys, Peter Njenga and George Waigwa, of Starehe Boys Centre and School in London in 1962, on the terrace of the House of Commons with two Members of Parliament, as part of the Youth Help Campaign to raise funds for the school (Photo by author from Starehe School archives)

Kariokor to Starehe. Through this merger, the duplication of some essential services was eliminated and the Kariokor building was converted into a dining hall for all the youths. This move formed the foundation of SBC as it is known today.

Early Challenges of Starehe Boys Centre and School

In the early years, despite the merger of the two youth clubs, fierce loyalty and rivalry between them made the migrants from Kariokor very upset. Some youths did not like the merger decision and caused an uproar, a situation that was immediately resolved by words of persuasion from Thomas Mboya. Mboya's help during SBC's formative years was phenomenal in enabling it to steady its foundations. He paid the school a visit in its earliest stages, and was both an astute supporter of its mission and work and its first patron. He served in the latter role until his sudden death in 1969.

Fig. 5.4 Cofounders of Starehe Boys Centre and School: Geoffrey Geturo, Joseph Gikubu, and Geoffrey Griffin (Photo by author from Starehe School archives)

Fig. 5.5 Opening of Starehe Boys Centre and School (Photo by author from Starehe School archives)

Encouraging youths to join the clubs and persuading local people to allow their sons to join was a tough undertaking in the beginning because of the African mistrust for Europeans in general and the colonial government in particular. A number of youths were not willing to join. It was thrust upon Gikubu to persuade the local people and African leaders, such as chiefs, to allow their sons to take part. Recalling these early difficulties, Gikubu noted:

> I went around Nairobi searching for the urchins in dirty streets, river banks, and factories. Some would come for a day or two and disappear. Others would come for only a few hours and sneak to town. Others disappeared along the way to Starehe. It was a desperate move getting youths to Starehe and Kariokor clubs and convincing them to stay.[12]

Fig. 5.6 Geoffrey Griffin at an early recruitment rally to encourage youths to join Starehe and Kariokor youth clubs (Photo by author from Starehe School archives)

Gikubu served as a translator of Griffin's message from English into Kiswahili and Gikuyu. Describing these early challenges, Roger Martin describes the following scene to demonstrate the reaction of African youths to early Gikubu and Griffin youth club recruitment rallies (Fig. 5.6):

> By now the crowd was two hundred strong and every eye was fixed on the speaker's serious, determined face. He seemed sincere, and the interpreter made his meaning quite plain; but Europeans did not offer such things to African children, neither did they venture unescorted into locations after dark. Clearly, this was some trick on the part of the government, though the idea behind it was obscure. The children hovering behind the group were cautious in their response. Before the speech was over, the vagrant boys who might have been taken away in the Land Rover were safely hidden in the long grass around the cemetery. The pale stranger and his assistant left empty-handed.[13]

Working at the school in its early days was tough and demanding. Most was accomplished by Griffin, Gikubu, and Geturo, the 17 boys who had joined SBC, and former staff and youths from Wamumu. The youths did not have adequate facilities such as a dining room, and each day they had to walk down to Kariokor Market for their meals. They also lacked bathrooms, and were required to use communal facilities in nearby housing estates. There were inadequate classrooms, workshops, administrative offices, and medical facilities. Any sick or injured youth had to be taken across Nairobi in Griffin's car to the hospital. The first uniforms were khaki shorts donated by the Prisons Department and cut down to fit the youths; there were no shoes or socks. Describing these enormous difficulties and the mammoth work that they did during this period, Gikubu noted (Fig. 5.7):

> We turned our hands to anything that needed to be done – teaching, building, cooking, mending fences, searching the city for runaways, guarding Starehe's meager property against robbers by night, and doing much of the

Fig. 5.7 Joseph Gikubu and Geoffrey Griffin in the early days of Starehe Boys Centre and School (Photo by author from Starehe School archives)

administrative work. There were no fixed working hours. We worked around the clock with minimal rest. Whatever work was required, we did it. It was hectic but we did it with joy. With time we won the youths' trust and with their support we were able to build a strong academic and affective record that gave us a name in Kenyan secondary education.[14]

In addition, the youths were not certain about their future, how long the founders of SBC would care for them, or the quality of education they were to receive from the institution. Needless to say, they were as wild as hawks, and it was extremely difficult to instill discipline in them. Some of them had suffered from the trauma of the loss of their parents during the Mau Mau War, others were sickly as a result of difficulties on the streets, and others were convicts from Makadara courts and were therefore perceived as criminals. Indeed, some of them thought SBC was an extension of prison and on many occasions ran away, deterred by the discipline and hard work that was required. Gikubu took an enormous amount of time to convince the youths of the importance of the clubs to their future. It took time before they developed confidence in him and SBC. Despite these difficulties, the youths built open-sided sheds for themselves to serve as the first classrooms and workshops for technical and artisan courses. Griffin begged for old corrugated iron sheets from the Kenya Prisons Department, which was being pulled down, and wood from Timsales Limited, to put up the first SBC buildings. With the help of Geturo, Gikubu, and the youths, within the first three months SBC began to offer a few trade courses under makeshift shades (Figs. 5.8 and 5.9).

There were no classrooms, teachers, or adequate staff to run SBC during its formative years. To solve this problem, Griffin invited any qualified artisans who wanted to make items for sale to use SBC's workshops as long as they taught the youths some form of trade. Using some of the little expertise in certain trades that he had learnt at Manyani and Wamumu, Gikubu assisted the artisans in teaching some of the trades and at the same time acted as a night watchman to guard the few assets of SBC that were being used for instruction or had been made by the youths. Other problems that they faced in the early years came from the inhabitants of SBC's neighboring estates, who viewed SBC as a security threat. Commenting on this, Gikubu noted:

> The reaction of our neighbors was hostile. They could not understand that these boys were in need of care and protection instead, they thought they

Fig. 5.8 Starehe Boys Centre and School early classrooms, made of tin and corrugated iron (Photo by author from Starehe School archives)

were criminals. They saw the club as a threat to their property, and were sure to blame us if a window was broken, or if something disappeared from a clothes-line. They would tell the staff that they were as bad as the youths and at one time they went to the District Officer and demanded that the club be removed. The unfortunate staff had to take turns in guarding stores and equipment by night not against Starehe's own youths, but against theft by covetous neighbors. The staff was often called on to look for youths who had been so intimidated by jeers and complaints from outside that they ran away. These were tough years for us.[15]

To overcome these initial difficulties, Griffin, Gikubu, and Geturo worked to instill self-confidence and pride in the youths. To them this was a battle which had to be won through good discipline and character irrespective of the hostility and difficulties that they were experiencing. They functioned as true parents, laboring to provide clothes, food, shelter, and education. Despite these early hurdles, the purposeful and constructive atmosphere proved increasingly attractive, especially to the many youths who were secretly longing to escape from the hopelessness of scavenging on

BUILT BY THE BOYS THEMSELVES, THIS BUILDING PROVIDED WORKSHOPS (WOODWORK, METALWORK, SIGN-WRITING AND CLAY MODELLING) AND CLASSROOMS. THE STUDY BLC NOW STANDS ON THE SAME GROUND.

Fig. 5.9 Starehe Boys Centre and School's early workshops for various trades (Photo by author from Starehe School archives)

the street. Most of them first came to the clubs through Elizabeth Jackson, the district officer at Makadara, well known for her kindness to those in need. This led slowly to steady development, starting with a move from the two tin huts to permanent buildings and the offering of programs that were continually improved upon. From the beginning, the aim of SBC was to rescue and rehabilitate vagrant and destitute youths, and in so doing combat juvenile delinquency—not by inaugurating a British-type recreational club but, rather, a training center for elementary academic and manual skills. Within a year, SBC had over 200 members, although the two tiny dormitories could only hold 60. This marked the beginning of its journey in Kenyan youth education.

Once these initial social problems had been addressed, Griffin, Gikubu, and Geturo decided to start a primary school, despite not having adequate structures in place or suitable teachers. The move faced strong opposition from the Ministry of Education. Recalling this, Gikubu observed:

The authorities thought we were mad! They wondered how this could be done without qualified teachers and proper classrooms! But we were adamant. When we started, we were not even allowed to call ourselves a school, we hid behind the name Starehe Youth Club. The City Council of Nairobi complained bitterly that we were breaking its by-laws but the critics left us alone when we told them to show us a better way of dealing with the problem. In fact, we invited them to take the youths away if they had any better ideas. But deep down our hearts, we knew they wouldn't do it. When they realized we weren't willing to relent, they learnt to condone the situation by pretending we didn't exist![16]

This marked the beginning of SBC—which basically started as an illegal school. It was here, using the experiences and the knowledge gained from Manyani and Wamumu, that Gikubu was destined to create a school that would rise to national and international fame. Although the founding of SBC was Griffin's personal initiative, neither he, Gikubu, nor Geturo foresaw the impact that this bold move into the unknown would make to Kenyan youth education in general. It was a leap of faith, with the hope that the little flower they were laboring to plant in the mud would grow and blossom. At this time, Kenya had a racially segregated system of education, one that favored the European and Asian populations in terms of finance, curricula, pedagogy, and structure. Most Africans still lacked adequate access to education both at primary and secondary levels. Many had their education terminated at the primary level. Commenting on this, Sorobea Bogonko writes:

> Throughout the 1950s, European children and Asian boys of ages, 7 to 15 had compulsory education. The Africans did not. Although they sat for separate preliminary examinations, European, and Asian children had continuous primary education up to Standard 7. African children, on the other hand, were pruned by the Standard 4 Common Entrance Examinations (CEE) and had to do four or three more years at the intermediate school before sitting for their preliminary examination. While the Kenyan European Preliminary Examination and the Kenyan Asian Preliminary Examination (KAPE) acted as qualifying examinations for secondary education, for Africans, KAPE was a school-leaving examination. Almost all the European and Asian pupils who finished primary education were admitted to secondary schools, but the successful African candidates were issued with a certificate which was considered a qualification for secondary education and for some type of training and direct employment. Throughout the 1950s and early 1960s, only 20 percent of African children proceeded to secondary school.[17]

By 1959, African KAPE candidates who proceeded to secondary school had risen to 28 percent. This meant that the number of dropouts at Standard Eight continued to be high, posing a major problem to those in authority. Although some dropouts found their way to trade schools, direct employment, or training centers for various jobs, as 1960 approached many had nowhere to go. The proposal to remove CEE or to increase the number of intermediate schools in order to allow all African schoolchildren to proceed to Standard Eight had proved to be just a dream. Whereas in 1954, 20 percent of the CEE candidates proceeded to intermediate schools, in 1956 and 1958 only 23 percent did so. Lack of funds, buildings, and staff were the limitations that made it impossible to provide intermediate education for all African children. The most important of these limitations was the half-heartedness with which the colonial government handled African education matters.[18] They thought of creating universal African educational standards for the first time in the 1957–1960 period, and money for education continued to be disproportionately allocated in favor of Europeans and Asians. It was not until 1962 that 80 percent of the CEE candidates found their way to intermediate schools. Around that time, almost all schools had seven or eight years of primary education. It was also in 1962 that expenditure on African education rose to 61 percent of the total money spent on education. Explaining Africans' lack of access to education during this period, Daniel Sifuna and James Otiende give the following figures in terms of school enrolments at both primary and secondary levels by 1963. At primary the figures were Africans 43.7 percent, Arabs 39.8 percent, Asians 77.5 percent, and Europeans 74.6 percent. In the secondary division, the figures were Africans 1.3 percent, Arabs 9.4 percent, Asians 80.0 percent, and Europeans 98.9 percent.[19] In addition, there were also few schools and inadequate learning facilities. In terms of curriculum and content, a basic education was offered, which was mainly labor-centered. These conditions drove the African demand for better education. Many began their own independent schools. But a lack of adequate educational opportunities offered to African youth resulted in vagrancy for many. This was worsened further with the declaration of the State of Emergency in 1952. Describing the high levels of youth vagrancy especially in Nairobi during this period, Griffin summarizes the situation in February 1962:

> The Ministry of Education reported a primary school enrolment of 653, 000 children, aged between 7 to 10 years. It was estimated that 119,000 children

in this age bracket were out of school. In the intermediate range between the ages of 11 to 14 years, 228,000 children were in school and about 438,000 were not! Of the estimated 600,000 children between 15 to 18 years, only a small percentage was in secondary school![20]

During this period Gikubu did not understand clearly the past experiences, the clear-sighted resolve, the driving force, the courage, and determination that had allowed Griffin to start SBC. To serve his aims, this school had to operate outside the country's educational system, with he himself deciding its rules, structure, and admission criteria. To succeed in his aims, he had to disguise his school as a club. Roger Martin observes that "only by disguising his new venture as a 'club' could he hope to avoid breaking the law or offending the government."[21] From the outset, Gikubu supported Griffin's efforts and urged him to ensure that they provided quality education for their students. He refused to concede to SBC's critics who saw it as an inferior school. Although it was different from mainstream institutions, Gikubu wanted the students to be able to hold their heads as high as any student from the best schools in Kenya. It was their initial aim to make SBC different from other youth clubs and schools patterned on British models. Gikubu remarked:

> From the beginning, we made up our mind that we would give quality parenting and the best education to the poor youths who came under our care. It was pointless to give the best care in the world if this was not matched by quality education, which could enable the boys to change their social standing. Passing exams very well was the only way they would get quality jobs and change their social status when they left school. Having lacked education in my life due to Mau Mau War, I knew it was the best weapon that would make our students successful in life.[22]

It was because of this grand plan that Gikubu was determined to play an intimate role in the life and development of the school. Although not a professionally trained educator and not highly educated himself, he was ready to use his previous educational experiences in Manyani and Wamumu, and to learn from educational experts' relevant approaches, in order to assist Griffin in establishing a strong academic institution. He was determined to succeed.

The early educational programs at SBC indicate Griffin, Gikubu, and Geturo's early interpretation of the Kenyans' basic needs at this time.

The students, given their backgrounds, required an in-depth education and varied skills that would enable them to function and succeed in the new and independent Kenyan state. Griffin, Gikubu, and Geturo argued that, although occupation was the key word, it was imperative to keep the students busy with useful activities that went far beyond the provision of recreational activities. They strived to offer elementary academic and manual skills, including literacy, carpentry, signwriting, tinsmithing, leatherwork, and all types of sports and games, especially boxing, scouting, drama, and singing. In addition, the students were given government trade tests to qualify them for adult employment. It was these modest provisions that Griffin, Gikubu, and Geturo set from the beginning to make their students relevant in the new Kenyan government; hence their determined struggle from the outset to change SBC from a youth club into a school. It is important to note that despite SBC's early progress, it continued to experience three major challenges in its first decade: lack of recognition as a school, the absence of social welfare, and political challenges.

Struggle for Recognition

Although SBC was on the right track, making slow but steady progress, the route to recognition took five years. Griffin, Gikubu, and Geturo battled with educational authorities to have the school registered, since it was initially viewed with grave suspicion. For instance, the Health Department and the city engineer were not impressed with its overcrowding and lack of approved facilities; the education officer was disturbed by SBC's attempts to masquerade as a formal school; the probation officer did not trust SBC's insistence on smart uniforms and a sense of corporate identity; the chief inspector of children objected to the lumping together of large numbers of apparently delinquent youths in substandard accommodation and an alarmingly "free" disciplinary regime. In addition, according to Peter Ojiambo, there was a fallacious belief that the intelligence levels of the vagrant youths who formed a great percentage of the SBC population were low and unsuited for academic work. No one believed that SBC could constitute an educational institution.[23]

Griffin, Gikubu, and Geturo understood very well from the beginning that they could not make any progress without a concrete building program, and in 1961 they pinned their hopes on the generous assistance of the Ford Foundation. Their urgent needs included living space and facilities for the boarders and more classrooms, as well as more staff to cater for the rapidly increasing number of students. The more they pressed for their registration, the more the Kenyan government hardened its stance. This began to create tension among the students and the few staff members. Griffin, Gikubu, and Geturo worked hard to convince staff and students alike of SBC's bright future, despite the difficulties they were experiencing.

In 1961, although SBC was given official recognition as a "continuation school" for students outside the mainstream national educational system, it was discouraged from following the primary school syllabus and was warned that its students were not going to be allowed to take preliminary examinations when they reached the equivalent of Standard Seven. This implied they could never gain a secondary school entry nor attain any qualification while at SBC, apart from the trade test that was meant for artisan employment. Other challenges that hampered the registration of the school by the Ministry of Education during this period were the staff members' inadequate qualifications, the poor quality of the classrooms, and a lack of sanitary facilities. The youth club nomenclature, with its provision for a transient and voluntary membership, was also not viewed with favor by the Ministry of Education. Because of these deficiencies, in 1963 the permanent secretary in charge of education permitted SBC to function only for a year, on condition that new buildings were constructed; if this did not take place, it would forfeit its registration.[24] Starehe did not have the huge sums of money that were required to build classrooms. To alleviate this situation, Griffin, Gikubu, and Geturo embarked on the construction of temporary structures using borrowed timber from Timsales Company, the Prisons Department, and donations from the provincial administration. It was during this period that the Oxford Committee for Famine Relief (Oxfam) came to their rescue, building the school's primary section (Fig. 5.10).

During this period, SBC ceased making excuses for the fact that it was drawing in students who should technically have been relocated in their home areas. Instead, it began thinking of its contribution to Kenyan youth education and the nation at large. It reasoned that such a mission was destined to fail if it had boundaries or admitted students based on their place of origin. It is in this regard that the Ministry of Education failure to register SBC as a primary school worried Griffin, Gikubu, and Geturo. They felt that the long-term solution to solving the students' problems was SBC's

Fig. 5.10 Starehe Boys Centre and School, built by Oxfam (Photo by author from Starehe School archives)

establishment of its own school to offer a sound education. According to Roger Martin:

> Starehe knew that education was highly prized in African society, and its provision would assist the school's remedial aims. Sending students out to ordinary schools, the normal practice of charitable institutions, was simply not good enough, the problems of fees, fixed entry dates, previous expulsions, emotional disturbance and possible provocation of teachers could only be properly resolved if Starehe educated its students on its own grounds and provided high quality education.[25]

In addition, they were concerned about what was to happen to their students if they were not given a proper education. This made them hold back some of the bright students for a year, with the hope that they would be allowed to take examinations in 1964. It was not easy to prepare these pioneer students for the Kenya Primary Examinations, and the Ministry of Education gave them stringent conditions to abide by. Despite this hurdle, SBC performed better than most of the registered schools owing to the determination of the volunteer teachers and students. Their success gave Griffin, Gikubu, Geturo, and the other SBC staff confidence to press forward with registration of the school's secondary section. Although Griffin, Gikubu, and Geturo were given tough conditions to fulfill, by early 1964 SBC was registered not only as a primary school but also as a secondary school, and was officially opened in September of the same year to serve in both capacities.

Social Welfare Challenges

During this period Starehe also faced challenges from the Social Welfare Department. It was accused of being inexperienced and lacking qualifications in the field. A powerful lobby within the colonial government protested that SBC was trespassing on the territory of approved schools and remand homes, and of using a sentimental approach to juvenile problems. The lack of order and supervision at SBC was interpreted as implying that it was leaning towards the idea of "free discipline." Bearing in mind that most of the students who were residing there were proven delinquent cases, it was seen as posing a security threat to the city's residents. In addition, SBC was accused of attempting to make "Etonians" out of destitute children.[26] Although SBC was supported by the officer in charge of provincial administration, the police, and several juvenile court magistrates, the feeling among "experts" within the colonial government was deeply held, and in late 1962 Griffin, Gikubu, and Geturo were confronted by the government, which gave them an ultimatum regarding educational activities. In its memo to Gikubu, who was in charge of boarding and student welfare, the Ministry of Home Affairs and Social Services advised:

> The best way to reduce the size of Starehe would be to remove some of the categories of students at present in training them, notably those on probation orders, those from outside Nairobi and all proven delinquents. This could be the first step, the long-term aim should be to turn away from the attempt to provide any form of actual education, and instead merely to supply occupation and past times for idle hands.[27]

This government directive was totally in opposition to all the accomplishments that Griffin, Gikubu, and Geturo had made in three years.

Moreover, it would not be easy to implement the suggested recommendations. Griffin, Gikubu, and Geturo's ideas differed extensively from those of the "experts." During this period, SBC was supported by John Nottingham, one of the earliest colonial officers to be interested in the problem of youth vagrancy (as noted earlier). Despite these challenges, Griffin, Gikubu, and Geturo were clear about what they were trying to do: it was something that few individuals were prepared to undertake, and there were minimal colonial structures in place to accomplish it. Further, it was practically impossible to gain admission to the few small and carefully controlled children's homes in Nairobi, and many students committed to approved schools were not in fact admitted.

It was not possible to reconcile Griffin, Gikubu, and Geturo to their adversaries because both parties had such differing views about how to address the juvenile delinquency problem. The colonial experts seemed to be more engrossed in theoretical attitudes towards care, correction, and education of the young, mainly deriving their stance from Britain, where resources were plentiful and education was free and compulsory. Their aim was to carry on their work within comfortable and manageable spaces, ignoring if necessary the actual conditions under which so many Kenyan youths were living at the time. Addressing the Kenyan Council of Social Services in 1961 in Nyasaland, and their inability to address the problem of youth vagrancy, Griffin gave a diagnosis of SBC's difficulties and the colonial educational realities of the time:

> I would like to ask you whether you are shooting at the right target. There are large groups of children who have no spokesman, probably 80 percent of the children of this country are not at school. I would like to ask what we are to do about the rest, who have no basic discipline or preparation for life, no school background and often no parental control either. We should go out and find these children, before it is too late.[28]

Griffin, Gikubu, and Geturo's criticism of the institutions in colonial Kenya was, first, that they tended to duck their primary obligation, which was to train youths for adult life in a harshly competitive society. They argued that even if they could not aspire to provide their own educational structure, they could take into account the contemporary Kenyan situation, rather than assuming there was a system of public education that would take care of all their requirements. They underscored the fact that government policy and the existing nongovernmental agencies failed to take advantage of the African extended family, which meant that practically every child had someone, somewhere, who would take an interest in him/her and provide adequate care. In their view, rules and regulations based on Western patterns were likely to deprive youths of the natural and precious right of community life. Addressing a child welfare seminar in Nairobi, Gikubu remarked: "we are in Africa! Let us use the social systems of Africa to solve youth vagrancy. Let us not bring exotic solutions in Africa that will not work! Let us not try to isolate the youth in an antiseptic island on which their relatives may not be allowed to see them!"[29]

Griffin, Gikubu, and Geturo did not trust the "love and affection" that was bestowed upon destitutes by most of the expatriates, who on the other hand were busy decrying institutional life. They saw education as the route through which the problem of youth vagrancy could be solved. Although it was a time-consuming and costly investment, they felt it was the only long-term solution.

Political Challenges

Although used to battling with authority, Griffin, Gikubu, and Geturo almost despaired in February 1961 when they were informed that Griffin's post in the Department of Community Development, and much of the rest of the department, was to be terminated because of economic reasons, and that he was to be deployed in the civil service at a junior rank, to continue his youth work in Nairobi and the countryside as a private citizen if he wished to do so. According to Kennedy Hongo and Jesse Mugambi, in essence Griffin was sacked, the reason being his involvement with an illegal institution—SBC. SBC was considered to be a youth club and therefore, under the rules of the Kenya Association of Youth Clubs, it was not recognized as an educational institution; thus, anything taking place there to do with learning activities was considered to be illegal.

Griffin, Gikubu, and Geturo understood the underlying opposition to their ideas in government circles, and the dilemma surrounding Griffin's employment as a government employee. As a private citizen with no standing in government, Griffin was likely to lose all power of independent action if it conflicted with established ideas. Because of this, his official title was changed to Colony Youth Organizer. However, the government decision was rescinded after various campaigns and a petition to the governor from his friends and supporters, especially Dorothy Hughes, who believed in the work that Griffin, Gikubu, and Geturo were doing in youth education.

There was also pressure from leaders of all races and political groups in Kenya who admired SBC's work.[30] Despite the political and social welfare challenges that they were facing, Griffin, Gikubu, and Geturo were undeterred, and were determined to see that SBC did not die. To enhance its educational work, Griffin apportioned his time between two offices, one in government and one at SBC. During this difficult period, Gikubu and Geturo did the bulk of the work in keeping SBC together, literally running the school between them. This went on for three decades—until 1988, when Griffin retired from his government position, his title having changed in 1964 to Director of the National Youth Service.

Establishing "A Place of Safety"

The last battle, and occasion for hostility and misunderstanding between SBC and the colonial government, took place as Save the Children Fund (SCF) was planning its new operations in Kenya in the early 1960s. To provide accommodation and security for youth vagrants in Nairobi, SCF intended to provide a transitional home, a "place of safety", before their final placement in families. The process of locating these families and arranging for the children's settlement, as well as providing school fees and other essentials, was long and complex, and a "transit home" of some sort was necessary. The dispute continued for a year, with Griffin, Gikubu, and Geturo's opponents insisting that concentrating large numbers of youths in a small area with inadequate supervision and "liberal discipline" was a risk to security. They were accused of using SBC as a refuge for criminal youths where they would plot further delinquent acts, and they were seen as delaying the delinquents' inevitable arrival in approved schools. Approved schools were seen by the colonial government as a better alternative. Responding to this criticism, and emphasizing SBC's sound approaches, which had low criminal activity in comparison with approved schools, Gikubu observed:

> In three and a half years, there had only been two instances, where a group of Starehe students had committed a crime together. This was probably a good record as that of any of Kenya's leading European schools. On the other hand, there had been reports within the last three years of approved school boys breaking out at night, robbing houses, smuggling drugs into schools and even growing it on the premises. The escape rate had also risen alarmingly and physical attacks on members of staff were becoming commonplace. We

refused to accept that approved schools, with their prison-like regime of confinement and poor educational standards were better than SCF noble vision.[31]

Despite this opposition, SBC received a lot of support and generous contributions from local firms. This enabled SCF Rescue Centre to open its doors for the first time in May 1961. Winning this battle excited Griffin, Gikubu, and Geturo: it had disproved the colonial government's argument that the only way to handle vagrant youths was to arrest them. The opening of the SCF Rescue Centre did not improve SBC's reputation in government circles, however. It was seen as confirming that SBC was attracting hardcore youth vagrants, delinquents, and innocent newcomers to the city. Critics saw the act of repatriation as having a statutory function that should be exercised by specific officials in accordance with a court order. This function was now being illegally usurped by a voluntary body. Despite these outbursts concerning SCF and its work, Griffin, Gikubu, and Geturo were confident that they were offering a Kenyan solution to a Kenyan problem. Their courageous refusal to bow to hostile colonial government authority was rewarded on March 4, 1963, with the inauguration of a new place of safety in SBC's grounds. This was intended to offer a more permanent base for youths under investigation and for those who could not be returned to their homes or had no homes to be returned to. Griffin was offered the position of an honorary administrator of SCF in Kenya.[32]

From the start Griffin, Gikubu, and Geturo were determined to give the youths who came under their care the best education possible. The two major handicaps they faced during this period were lack of money and the right personnel. They knew that with time both of these would be overcome. They began putting systems in place to strengthen their role. Reflecting on their faith during this period, Gikubu noted: "with a strong foundation to stand on, we knew the sky would be the limit. With the students and teachers on our side we knew we could succeed despite the challenges we were experiencing."[33] In 1961, SBC received special donations from the African Trust Fund and Nairobi Round Table No. One, which enabled it to built its first permanent structures. Soon after, it received support from SCF, which had an enormous effect on its financial stability for over three decades. The SCF met almost all SBC's expenditure, including students' sponsorship and the hiring of teachers during this period.

SBC's Educational Work in the Postcolonial Period

The postcolonial educational activities of Griffin, Gikubu, and Geturo at SBC were a historical phase that entailed SBC's recognition as a school and the evolution of its programs to meet Kenyan needs. This reflects wider Kenyan educational efforts and the search for an effective education system that fostered its developmental goals. After independence, Griffin, Gikubu, and Geturo felt secure owing to the confidence that the new independent Kenyan government showed in their educational work. The Kenyan government provided not only land but also some aid in the form of a teaching faculty. This support confirmed all that Griffin, Gikubu, and Geturo had been fighting for during the last years of colonialism. In mid-1964, they seemed to have reached the end of a long and weary road. They were assured of governmental support, and SBC's reputation stood high both at home and abroad. At this time, its first crop of candidates for the Kenya Preliminary Examinations were wondering what the future had in store for them, in terms of their secondary education and SBC's ability to fund it. The Youth Help Campaign had illustrated how limited the resources of Kenyan charities were. There was thus an urgent need for help if their plans to establish a strong secondary school were to materialize. During this critical period, there was a visit from Dr. Mulock Houwer, Secretary-General of the International Union for Child Welfare. His short article in the Union's Newsletter in the latter part of 1964 served not only to reinforce SBC's principles but also led to a generous flood of international funding that was beyond all expectations. He described SBC as the best example of a private initiative addressing issues of youth vagrancy that he had ever seen in a developing country. He called it a model project that deserved funding. It was "'a flower in the mud' – an institution with an astonishingly efficient and dynamic avant-garde approach, in fact, a model project for Africa."[34]

This led to massive capital grants in the following years, transforming SBC into a gigantic institution with a clear academic purpose and a momentum of its own, overwhelming Griffin, Gikubu, and Geturo's earlier expectations. Among the key donors during this period were Oxfam, the Nuffield Foundation, Mrs. Walter Kerr, the Danish government, the Danish Scouts Help Organization, the Bernard Van Leer Foundation, the Netherlands government, the International Union for Child Welfare, Blue Peter, the German Protestant Central Agency for Development, Netherlands Comite voor Kinderpostzegels, and the British, Norwegian, and Danish SCF. The

Kenyan government reacted positively to this international generosity. The Lands Department gave SBC a 99-year land lease on both the old and new sites, with a nominal rent. It approved most of the building plans in record time and added acres of land on the racecourse site. The rapid growth, beyond what Griffin, Gikubu, and Geturo had anticipated, was viewed by them as a miracle. They strongly believed that it was proof that God was involved in SBC's work. Supporting this belief, Gikubu observed (Figs. 5.11, 5.12, and 5.13):

> We have been struck in time and again with the manner in which one door opens as another closes. We reach the end of one phase of development, and have no idea at all how anything further can be attempted. Yet after no more than a breathing space, a chance meeting or a casual contact sets us off again. One or two such happenings might be dismissed as coincidence, but not when they occur over and over again. My personal belief is that any scheme for the

Fig. 5.11 A visit by Indira Gandhi to Starehe Boys Centre and School (Photo by author from Starehe School archives)

Fig. 5.12 The visit by Princess Anne to Starehe Boys Centre and School (Photo by author from Starehe School archives)

needy receives something special by way of divine intervention for just as long as the people concerned work to the limits of their abilities.[35]

SBC's growth during this period was guided by its efficient, transparent, accountable, and dedicated administrative and teaching staff, who were led by Griffin, Gikubu, and Geturo. Despite the numerous challenges they experienced during this period, their vision and unwavering purpose were essential to SBC's growth and success. They worked to the limits of their abilities and gave their all. In later years, owing to Griffin, Gikubu, and Geturo's emphasis on forming strong ties with their staff, SBC was able to attract committed administrators, many of whom arrived initially as foreign volunteers. They greatly assisted SBC in setting up strong educational systems. Among the key early volunteers were Roger Martin and Patrick Shaw. However, despite this, as new generations flooded in each January, the staffing situation seemed to deteriorate. The Ministry of Education had increased its official "establishment" to six grant-aided posts by now; but for

Fig. 5.13 A visit by Bishop Desmond Tutu to Starehe Boys Centre and School (Photo by author from Starehe School archives)

much of 1968 five of these posts were unfilled, largely because SBC, unlike other government secondary schools, had no housing for expatriates with families. Even after they left SBC some of these early volunteers remained in touch, and they have been strong ambassadors in its financial campaigns overseas. One of the early British volunteers who has remained close is Paul Whitehouse, who came to SBC in the early 1960s. At the time of writing he is the chair of Starehe United Kingdom Association, which comprises former Starehe volunteer teachers. Other devoted expatriates who provided fruitful labor and were devoted to SBC during these early years included Peter Attenborough, Sister Linda, Rex Roberts, Don Lowreys, Roger Beeneys, Sister Christiana, Vera Lewins, Andrew Passey, Donald Lamb, Rodney Bendon, Christopher Read, Erik Nielsen, Ramilla Ruparel, Bill Owen, and Ciciliama Puttanickal.[36] It was upon their shoulders that SBC cemented its foundation and growth. Despite this progress, Griffin,

Gikubu, and Geturo faced two other major challenges during this period: staffing and administrative difficulties.

Staffing Difficulties

Griffin, Gikubu, and Geturo insisted on seeking African teachers, for it was their belief that an Africanized staff would provide continuity in teaching as opposed to a seasonal expatriate staff. However, their efforts to secure local staff were met with numerous setbacks. The teachers' reliability was uncertain, and there was approximately 50 percent turnover every year among both the Kenyan teachers and the expatriates. Some of the local difficulties with regard to recruitment were caused by the ease with which well-educated Kenyans could find well-paid jobs during this period. Explaining the desperate situation during this period, Peter Ojiambo recounts the following story: "a Kenyan science graduate teacher resigned after one term. Another teacher was posted to Starehe on completion of his Makerere Education degree, arrived, took one look round and resigned on the spot."[37]

Owing to these difficulties, the secondary division was forced to depend excessively on its volunteer staff, an admirable thing from the standpoint of energy, morale, and extracurricular activity but less so where continuity and efficiency of school work was concerned. The staffing problems affected the performance and continuity of learning in some subjects. The sixth form, for instance, suffered most especially in English, history, and geography, where the turnover was very high. By 1971, geography had virtually collapsed because the only member of staff who was remotely capable of teaching it had been interdicted. Prior to 1973, appointing teachers in the first place was difficult enough, but their incessant and often unexpected departures were frustrating.[38] A few left because of disaffection, usually because the member of staff concerned could not accept or work within the SBC management structure, which was authoritarian. Commenting on this, Elizabeth Pamba noted: "Griffin, Gikubu, and Geturo were too strict at the beginning and they found out that they were losing many teachers. When teachers did not want to engage in an argument with them, they asked for transfer."[39]

Despite these difficulties, there was, however, no possibility of removing an incompetent teacher from the SBC staff, even when criticisms of SBC reached dangerous proportions. In principle, the Ministry of Education had promised to gradually build up the posts in both secondary and technical divisions until all the essential teaching staff were paid by the government;

but every New Year SBC faced the same protracted rigmarole of queried estimates, mislaid letters, and accusations that there were too many staff. More than once Griffin, Gikubu, and Geturo were compelled to break through the red tape by going straight to the top with a plea for urgent action, since the granting of a post was only the first step; then intent had to be registered; and securing an expatriate for the job after this took another year. In the end, everything was always arranged and the teaching staff increased by about six posts each year. But the negotiations for a given year were not always completed before the first approaches for the following year had to be made.[40]

In 1973, Griffin, Gikubu, and Geturo saw a breakthrough with regard to established posts, when the Ministry of Education finally agreed to a planned annual increase, climbing to a full establishment of 40 teachers for the two divisions in 1975. During this time, the Van Leer Foundation bridged the gap with a final grant of £7,500; and in 1976, after a reassessment, the number of government posts was increased to 47, while the assistant directors in charge of each division became eligible for school principals allowance. This seemed to imply that from now on the volunteer teaching help could be regarded as an additional luxury, whose work would enrich SBC but without which it could survive. The practical situation on the ground, however, was different, because an established post was of no use unless it was filled with a teacher. Describing the reality, Griffin noted that "for months in 1974 several forms had to go without mathematics teaching. To resolve the situation, Starehe was forced to recruit a teacher and pay him using its own funds."[41]

Despite these teething staffing problems, the students accepted the situation calmly. The adverse effects over the years were outweighed by the fruitful labors of a spirited, devoted, and dedicated team of both Kenyan and expatriate teachers under the leadership of Griffin, Geturo, and Gikubu. It was upon these strong pillars that SBC built its academic excellence.

Administrative Difficulties

During SBC's formative years, the secondary division had a heavy leadership turnover, but despite this examination results were not disastrous. By 1972, the school had a sound administrative system and steadily improving examination outcomes, as well as encouraging academic responses from the students. The stature of the staff had increased greatly, although according to Roger Martin the school still suffered from "poisonous" and "destructive" staff room gossip which criticized SBC's integrity, this threatening at times to tear the school apart. It seemed that only the passing of time, and the growing collective maturity of the staff, could resolve this problem.[42] This latter was greatly enhanced with the arrival of Raphael Wanjohi in January 1972 to assist Griffin, Gikubu, and Geturo. He managed to bring a magnificent serenity of temperament together with real firmness of purpose to bear on his work, and students and teachers responded well to his administrative style. However, he was suddenly transferred to Eastleigh Secondary School as headmaster. He was succeeded by David Hunter, who only lasted one term, leaving to become principal of Friends' College at Kaimosi. He was replaced by the Rev. Bill Owen, who championed the academic success of SBC for more than four years.

During this period of rapid change, Griffin, Gikubu, and Geturo ensured that there was basic continuity in the running of the school. They did this by keeping strongly on top of disciplinary issues and by strengthening and empowering various heads of departments through the formation of a Board of Studies, which was charged with enhancing SBC's academic standards. Further, despite their heavy administrative schedules they took a close personal interest in the most minor aspects of SBC's daily life, its educational work, vision, and mission. It is this grip that allowed them to improve SBC academically, as evidenced in the programs that were undertaken from 1974 onwards: technical education, accountancy, and computer studies, alongside the expansion of SBC's secondary and tertiary education.

Technical Education

In 1965 two streams were established: secondary and secondary-technical. These were run concurrently, unlike other Kenyan schools which had one of the two. Griffin, Gikubu, and Geturo's decision to offer both was guided by their vision of the future needs of their students, based on their deprived socio-economic backgrounds, their academic abilities, and Kenya's labor policies, which emphasized the importance of a skilled workforce. Since a majority of SBC's students came from deprived environments, Griffin, Gikubu, and Geturo wanted to ensure that those students who could not excel in the mainstream secondary division or those who had uncertain academic abilities would excel in the technical education section. Until January 1966, SBC's technical division comprised students who had no clear academic talents and whose aim was to pass the Ministry of Labor Trade Test for artisans. Despite its overall success, the division worked within a limited sphere, and this became clear when the secondary school was formed.[43] Griffin, Gikubu, and Geturo utilized the richer opportunities that were given by the Oxfam technical building to train students in courses that could enable them to sit for the Kenya Junior Secondary (Technical) examinations. This gave students a qualification in basic academic subjects and a sound basis in engineering techniques, technical drawing, and workshop skills, which enhanced their employment opportunities after secondary education was complete. The students learned motor mechanics, metalwork, carpentry, and signwriting. Although the Oxfam workshops were ready for use, there was a grave shortage of equipment, vital tools, and teachers, which made practical work difficult. For these reasons Griffin, Gikubu, and Geturo abolished the stream, and students were absorbed into the secondary division in 1967.

In 1969, with the building of workshops, it was possible to enlarge the division to enable it to run well. With these greatly improved facilities, engineering, motor mechanics, and technical courses were added. It was now possible to run a three-year Kenya Junior of Secondary Education (KJSE) technical course, and this led to the recruitment of a new form in 1969, under the full control of the technical division. Despite this progress, SBC still feared the future availability of qualified staff to run the program without expatriate volunteers' support. Even with its new workshops, the division labored under great hardships in terms of classroom space and adequate faculty. The situation improved in 1970 with the intake of a higher caliber of "vocational" engineering classes, the practical and experienced approach of Bill Glover, the division's new head, improved supplies of materials and equipment, and the success with which the artisan students were securing jobs after their training was complete. The national importance of this division was emphasized by Education Permanent Secretary James Gacathi, when he visited SBC in March 1970. He noted that the country possessed 800 secondary schools but few technical training institutions, and that it was a vital issue of policy that students should learn "to use their hands as well as their heads."[44]

By 1973, the second Netherlands building was opened, and the division moved entirely to a new section of the school. The old "artisan" courses were phased out. The trade tests were viewed as not being a reliable measure and, with a more competitive labor market, the Grade III Test was not an assurance of employment. Although most of the students made a fair showing at the Kenya Junior Secondary Examinations, the Grade III test was abolished in 1972, immediately after the pioneer "vocational" class had sat for it and the students obtained permission to do the basic engineering examination of City and Guilds, which the government abolished before the candidates sat for it. This required their staying on for a year to finish the course, a move that led to the birth of SBC's first Technical Form IV. Starehe's technical division was unique, and it was one of the country's few technical schools that was fully fledged and well equipped enough to offer a full secondary technical course.[45] The abolishment of the basic engineering examination of City and Guilds led to the introduction of its equivalent qualification, the East Africa Certificate of Education (EACE) Technical, which was to become mandatory for all technical schools. This meant that SBC's students who might have been "good with their hands" but lacked aptitude for academic work were now required to undertake examinations in English, mathematics, science, and general subjects, which were equivalent to Secondary EACE.

After the technical division had been introduced by the Ministry of Education, Griffin, Gikubu, and Geturo realized that the division could no longer be a place of refuge for Certificate of Primary Education (CPE) failures, and that none of the students would be admitted to the Technical Form unless they had demonstrated an ability to pass the secondary division entrance exam. This did not solve SBC's dilemma about was to happen to those students who had failed in SBC's primary school, those many students with unhappy backgrounds who simply could not be prematurely thrown into a hostile world. To solve this predicament, they designed a temporary measure, introducing elementary Pitman courses in English, mathematics, and book-keeping, together with the old Grade III Trade Test. As in the past, they sought to find jobs for their students upon completion of school.[46] To facilitate this, they established the Starehe General Engineering Co-operative Society Limited in 1978. This sought to create a steady income for the school, in addition to employing and training a certain number of SBC's school leavers each year in technical and commercial skills. Although it had a short existence, it was effective in meeting SBC's objectives at the time. A commerce course was also introduced, lasting a year and three months, which prepared students for the Accounts Clerks Examination of the Kenya National Secretaries and Accountants Board. This was meant to provide a valuable qualification for their professional employment.

Griffin, Gikubu, and Geturo were opposed to the government's phasing out of technical education. They saw it as a vital avenue for students who did not make it to university and as an essential source of skilled personnel. Commenting on their views on technical education, Edith Karaimu, a long-serving teacher and administrator at SBC, observed: "they (Griffin, Gikubu, and Geturo) were great advocates for the middle level technical colleges. They saw them as the radius of Kenya's development."[47] Commenting further on the value of technical education and middle-level colleges to the growth of SBC, Griffin observed that Kenya's educational planning had to focus sharply on the expansion of middle-level institutions, partly because of the growing number of students who were unable to gain entry to university, and the fact that universities were already satisfying high-level personnel demands. He argued:

> We need to be flexible and constantly evaluate training at tertiary level so as to redress deficiencies in terms of skills which are in short supply and reappraise disciplines whose skills are abundant and therefore not an immediate priority. It all boils down to rationalizing educational training to match labor demands. Emphasis must be focused on the type and nature of education, which will ultimately produce individuals who can be effectively absorbed into the job market and hence improve economic growth.[48]

Accountancy and Computer Studies

The period between 1973 and 1981 saw SBC improve and reshape its academic programs to enable it to meet the country's demands. This period marked its permanent position among the top ten secondary schools in Kenya and the phasing out of its high school technical section. It was during this time that Griffin, Gikubu, and Geturo took a great leap in introducing post-secondary school training programs, specifically, accounting. Initially, the school offered only Accounts Clerk National Certificate courses, which were low-level accountancy training courses, but in 1983 it introduced higher level certified public accountancy courses. In 1988, with the introduction of the new system of education, 8-4-4, which came about because of the educational policy reforms of the 1980s and was instituted to address unemployment difficulties experienced by both primary and secondary graduates in Kenya, Griffin, Gikubu, and Geturo undertook a further reshaping of SBC's academic programs to meet these new changes. They started a post-secondary institute to offer two-year accountancy and computer courses. The latter was funded by the Austrian government, although it had been introduced to the school much earlier. Accountancy courses were also raised to the second level in this period. The two courses blended well with SBC's old programs. They were introduced mainly to train those students who did not qualify for a university education. Commenting on the rationale for their introduction, Peter Okono, who had been the head of the program for several years, noted:

> Griffin, Gikubu, and Geturo's initiative in setting up a computer and accounts college was a natural response to the question of those students who fail to gain university admission but are obviously capable of pursuing further education to enable them get gainful employment. They argued that postsecondary education must be geared towards ensuring that the students pursue skills, which can adequately prepare them for the job market so that they can meaningfully participate in national development.[49]

Focusing on the future demands of Kenyan society, Griffin, Gikubu, and Geturo sought to expand SBC's secondary and institute education. This meant phasing out the primary section of the school in the early 1990s and investing more at secondary and tertiary levels. They realized that with the introduction of Free Primary Education (FPE), Universal Primary Education (UPE), and the global advocacy of Educational for All (EFA) there were other groups taking care of basic primary education both at governmental and nongovernmental level. They saw a future high demand for secondary and tertiary education. Affirming the global education demands during this period and their impact on secondary education, Daniel Sifuna and James Otiende observe that global market competition, growing access to primary education, and new information technology created a fast-growing demand for more and better secondary education services in developing countries. Expansion of secondary education was seen as vital for faster industrialization. This was evidenced in the increase in developing countries' secondary school gross enrolments during this period. For instance, with industrialization, the newly industrialized countries of Korea, Malaysia, and Mauritius had achieved secondary school gross enrolment ratios of 42 percent, 34 percent, and 30 percent respectively by the early 1980s. By 1991, these ratios had risen to 88 percent, 58 percent and 54 percent compared with Kenya's 29 percent.[50] It was within this frame of thinking that Griffin, Gikubu, and Geturo strived hard to increase SBC's investment in secondary and tertiary education. This constant reinvigoration of the courses made SBC one of the leading partners in Kenyan youth education for several decades. Starehe was among the first schools in Kenya to offer computer and accountancy programs, and it is not surprising that there are many SBC old students at the forefront of information technology and business-related sectors in the country.

The Establishment of SBC, and Its Reflection of Kenya's Educational History in the Postcolonial Period

The establishment of SBC in the postcolonial period reflects Kenya's educational historical context and its legacy. This phase presents the growth of SBC from two tin huts into a modern complex institution. Starehe's rapid growth during this period confirms Dr. Mulock Houwer's earlier-cited quote that indeed it "was a flower in the mud." It was a flower that was able to surmount several challenges with regard to its infrastructure, and academic programs to blossom. This phase shows the educational growth of SBC in terms of its struggles to be recognized as a school and the opposition it faced from the Ministry of Education; its final registration in 1964; and the difficulties it faced in its early decades with regard to finances, classrooms, workshops, teachers, facilities, low academic levels, and continuous reviews of its educational programs. In addition, we also see the current historical educational position of SBC and how it has been negotiating its educational difficulties and equipping its students with necessary skills that are required for Kenya's development.

The inadequate educational institutions, facilities and personnel that were a feature of Kenya at the time of its independence reflect the colonial educational structure of the time. These are evidenced in SBC's challenges. It was difficult for SBC to recruit Kenyan teachers despite its constant requests to the Ministry of Education. Varied reasons accounted for this, including the new and promising jobs that were offered to early African graduates and the limited training opportunities provided by the colonial government for African teachers. Thus, at the dawn of independence, the Kenyan government had urgently to find more trained African teachers for the numerous new schools that were being built to accommodate the large Kenyan school age population that had no access to education prior to independence: this was a daunting task. This expansion had not been adequately planned for and it created new staffing challenges. The spillover effects of this crisis were later felt at secondary level, owing to the increased number of primary school graduates. For these reasons, in the mid-1970s the Kenyan government began a recruitment program to employ untrained teachers in order to ease the problem.

The findings bring to the fore the new Kenyan government's replication of colonial methods of school registration. This is seen in its strict regulations around the registration of new schools, which required them to have sufficient space for classrooms, as well as adequate teachers, textbooks, and buildings. Although this might have been a good move for keeping track of the quality of education that was being offered, the process of approval took too long and imperiled a society that was in dire need of a standard of education that few existing schools were able to provide. Starehe's constant reinvigoration of its educational programs during the postcolonial period reflects Kenya's educational evolution and its struggles to foster national development.

Between 1959 and 1962, SBC engaged more in artisan courses—literacy, carpentry, signwriting, tinsmithing, and leatherwork. These were "transitional courses" that were meant to give students quick skills that could allow them to function in society. The years after independence brought great hope to Africans who had suffered discrimination in all spheres of life during colonial rule, especially in the field of education. Colonial education was structured along racial lines, with Africans getting the least advantage in the system. In the period 1963 and 1971 Kenya was confronted with a very great shortage of skilled workers to run its economy. Education was viewed as a gateway to training the required workforce, and this was the central objective of the government's Sessional Paper Number 10 of 1965 and the Ominde Commission, which formulated the new education policy. Education was seen much more as an economic rather than a social service, a key means of alleviating the shortage of domestic skilled workers and a vehicle for creating equal economic opportunities for all citizens. The organization of education was closely linked to the management of human resources and labor market needs.[51] These were the objectives that formed the framework of Kenya's First and Second Developmental Plans of 1964/1970, and 1970/1974. After independence, the main concerns of most African education systems were how to create national consciousness, train adequate personnel, address societal needs, enhance quality, and improve access to education. This foresight is evidenced in Griffin, Gikubu, and Geturo's high emphasis on technical education, which was vital for Kenya's developmental growth.

For SBC to fit into this postcolonial education plan, its founders strived to change it from a club to a school, so that its students could attain the technical skills that were required to build the new nation. Immediately after registration as a school, SBC begun two wings of education, as previously noted: technical and secondary, both aimed at enabling its graduates to meet the demands of the new independent state.

Starehe's lack of teachers, equipment, and workshops for its technical division is a reflection of the wider Kenyan difficulties that most technical schools were experiencing at the time. It indicates the scarce government resources which impeded the fulfillment of its technical education requirements. The government's efforts to invest more in secondary education during this period were influenced by the human capital theory, which led to the growth in secondary school enrolments. This rapid growth continued to be experienced in the 1980s. Education was seen as a vehicle for individual mobility and a good life. Although education seemed to be expanding drastically at this time, its expansion did not equate to the country's economic growth. Therefore, most school dropouts were soon left without jobs or training. By 1970, secondary school dropouts began to experience unemployment.

In 1975, the government realized that its education system was not meeting its objectives. According to Daniel Sifuna and James Otiende, "most secondary school dropouts still preferred being employed in offices as clerks, secretaries or managers."[52] These were perceived as prestigious jobs compared with technical, mechanical, and agricultural jobs. Because of these educational difficulties, the International Labor Organization (ILO) started calling for changes in the education system, and it is in this context that the Kenyan Third Developmental Plan of 1974/1978 emphasized the effective utilization of human resources and further development of appropriate skills at all levels of education. The education system was required to produce, among other things, the high-level skills that were required for economic and industrial growth. To meet these demands, the plan advocated for the introduction of vocational/technical training programs as well as the promotion of appropriate attitudes favorable to development. In addition, it sought to make education more beneficial to both the individual and the nation. The plan laid emphasis on education's practical and technical components.

To address the problem of wastage during this period, the Kenyan government placed emphasis on technical education so that those who were not able to go on with secondary education could receive training that led them either to self-employment or granted them jobs in the nonformal sector. A critical examination of SBC's programs during this period indicates more investment and increases in donor funding for its tertiary technical section and the phasing out of the technical wing of secondary education. These changes were aimed at ensuring that SBC graduates would meet the needs of Kenya's Third Developmental Plan and were able to gain employment.

In 1976, the National Committee on Educational Objectives and Policy (Gacathi Report) was formed. This emphasized the provision of free primary education. The report observed that secondary education should be integrated with the nonformal sector so as to cater for school dropouts and unemployment challenges. It recommended the introduction of more technical subjects in secondary education. It sought to restructure the education system to enable it to meet the demands of the country and to prepare students adequately for the labor market. It also endeavored to address issues of quality, relevance, and equity. The report laid more emphasis on prevocational, technical, and practical education. Starehe's response to these demands was to expand its technical division further. It also introduced a commerce course and expanded its accountancy program.

The 1980s witnessed a change in governmental educational policies. It sought to address employment difficulties, which were still being experienced by both primary and secondary school graduates. As early as the 1970s, the ILO report had shown that changes had to be made to education to help reduce unemployment, and recommended increasing technical aspects of education. There were also proposals from the United Nations (UN) and World Bank that pertained to the educational plans for most Third World countries that had attained independence in the 1960s and 1970s. The UN proposal focused on the production of a skilled workforce, on reducing social inequalities, and on providing basic education for all. The ILO proposal for vocationalizing education was supported by the World Bank. This led to the establishment of technical and vocational training centers in Kenya with financial assistance from developed countries. The International Development Agency (IDA) was instrumental in spearheading the logistical funding of equipment that was required by various secondary schools across the country. This forced the Kenyan government to change the educational approach that had existed since independence. The government sought to establish an educational system that would make Kenyan citizens self-reliant. To effect this, a Presidential Working Party was formed in 1981 (Mackay Commission) to explore the possibilities. Its purpose was to enable youth to play a more effective role in the life of the nation by giving them the necessary skills, knowledge, and attitudes that were required for work and social development. The Mackay Commission recommended the establishment of a second Kenyan university geared towards vocational courses and societal development.[53] It underscored the need for education to address national development objectives, and gave rise to the current Kenyan 8-4-4 system. Education under this commission was designed to provide lifelong skills, and to make individuals self sufficient, productive in agriculture, industries, and commerce.

To meet the objectives and demands of the new system of education and to improve the quality of its graduates, unlike other Kenyan schools SBC started a postsecondary diploma institute to offer accountancy and computer courses. It also became affiliated to Jomo Kenyatta University of Agriculture and Technology in mid 1990s to offer a diploma in computer studies. The purpose of this was to prepare its students adequately for the immediate and future dialectical demands of the Kenyan labor market. In addition, it begun offering its own internally designed and examined diploma in information technology. The purpose of this was to enable students from SBC to study a three-year instead of a four-year degree program in information related fields. In these courses, Griffin, Gikubu, and Geturo's focus was always on quality rather than quantity.

In this chapter, although I have discussed Gikubu's work in Kenyan youth education through his work at SBC, his work at this time was very much intertwined with his close working relationship with and the mission and vision of Griffin and Geturo. Although they worked as a team, they each played their own individual parts to shape SBC's growth and influence on Kenyan youth education. In the following section, I would like to discuss briefly Gikubu's specific work at SBC.

The Roles that Gikubu Played at SBC

In the early years of SBC, Gikubu was in charge of the school selection process. He toured various parts of Kenya to recruit disadvantaged students who wanted to join the school. He was successful in this work and adept at uncovering fraudulent applications, as illustrated by this example given by Roger Martin: "the headmaster of a primary school, who secured admission for his own son on the carefully-documented plea that the boy was fatherless, was caught by Gikubu and taken to court for providing false admission to the school."[54] Among his other duties was to serve as a housemaster from 1965 to 1969. Starehe's house system, according to Roger Martin, worked well owing to "Gikubu's diligence, excellence, hard work, good relationship with students, the support of the staff and his good humor."[55] He carried a real weight of responsibility and did the bulk of the work in the boarding section. In 1969, he was appointed Assistant Director (Boarding), with full control of the entire boarding section of over 1,200 students. As SBC never closes and students must be cared for 365 days a year, these responsibilities far exceeded anything in an ordinary boarding school. They included finance, management of stores, personnel, and all aspects of student welfare and discipline. His labors over so many years and efficiency in management were fundamental to the discipline and growth of SBC over five decades. They enabled it to rise rapidly from a tiny school to a major national and international institution. In the first two decades of the school, although the turnover of assistant directors in the teaching division was high, the main office led by Gikubu remained intact. It did the work of a battalion, and of its devotion to SBC's work there was no doubt.

Among the most notable activities that Gikubu engaged in at SBC beyond the administrative work that became his hallmark were athletics and the physical training display. The latter won SBC a lot of national awards and international acclaim. Its dexterity and beauty, according to King'ala, saw SBC invited to numerous national celebrations, including Kenya's first independence celebrations and later its tenth anniversary:

> December 1973, saw the celebration of the tenth anniversary of Kenya's independence. The physical team returned to the stadium, where it had performed at the independence ceremony in 1963. They gave an immaculate performance. The President thanked Gikubu for his leadership and Starehe for its excellence in academics and extra-curricular activities. He noted with gratitude their first appearance during the first independence celebration in 1963 when they were just a small school.[56]

The SBC's physical training team under Gikubu's leadership became a national sensation, and for several decades it was invited to numerous agricultural shows throughout the country:

> For the first time, the team left Nairobi in 1974 to give their display to provincial audiences. At the Eldoret, Nakuru and Kisumu shows tremendous enthusiasm was generated. The Kisumu District Commissioner later came to Starehe to present 70 pounds as a gesture of appreciation for its excellence in extra-curricular activities.[57]

Writing a letter to Gikubu, recognizing his role in physical training and the fame it had brought to SBC, Griffin wrote on October 8, 1974:

> Just a line to put on record my delight and admiration for all your efforts at the recent Nairobi Show and in particular, for the enormous success of the physical education display. This display has now won every laurel open to it in Kenya, and has proved a triumph of faith and zeal on your part. Its effects in exciting public admiration for Starehe are immense. I would like you to know that I really appreciate all that you have done. Every day you keep confirming to me that we were right in starting Starehe.[58]

Upon Griffin's death in 2005, although he was long overdue for retirement, Gikubu was appointed acting school director, a position he served in until 2007 when the new director was appointed. He was retained in service to oversee the leadership transition. Although this was a heavy role to play, he managed to sustain SBC's harmony and high academic standards, and for two years he guided the new director. In early 2009, the trustees again bestowed upon him the role of acting director upon the departure of the new principal, a role he played with remarkable success until November 2009, when a youthful and highly qualified director was appointed. Gikubu's role during this transition period was to ensure that SBC's mission, vision, values, academic standards, and cocurricular standards remained strongly entrenched. He would have continued to serve as the director of SBC but he felt that a much younger and more educated person should lead the school. He argued: "Starehe of now is not the Starehe of 1959. The present Starehe requires fresh blood, vision, energy, and new academic and co-curricular programming that can enable it build on its current success."[59]

Gikubu returned to his assistant director in charge of boarding position, a role he held until his death in 2014. Asked whether he contemplated retiring given that he was approaching 80 years of age, he responded, "a father never retires from his family. You are always permanently there to guide and advice. The process never ends. Starehe is my family and I will always be there for it, to guide it, and offer my services whenever needed."[60] During his tenure as director, Gikubu managed to forge a strong academic and cocurricular institution that was pragmatic, holistic, and service centered. Summing up his overall passion for youth education over the years, he noted: "education that is worthy must transform people's lives. It must change and reconstruct society. It cannot afford to be an education for education's sake. This has been my mission at SBC for the last 55 years."[61] For his service and contributions to Kenyan youth education, Gikubu was awarded Moran of the Order of the Burning Spear and Head of State Commendation honors by the government on December 12, 1987.

In summary, this chapter illustrates that the founding of SBC reflects Kenya's educational context both in the colonial and postcolonial periods. Through the founding of SBC, Kenya's educational struggles over the years are reflected, and the efforts to reform its educational system to enable it to engage with myriad societal challenges are made clear. Additionally, the founding and growth of SBC reflect Kenya's efforts to reshape its national character through the educational process. It can be deduced that a critical examination of SBC's spiral educational programs over the years provides insights on the future shape and form of Kenya's high school and tertiary education. It reveals the challenges and necessary resources that can make the country's graduates relevant to its developmental agenda. By and large, a historical overview of education in Kenya that is reflected in the founding and growth of SBC shows certain, almost definite, social, cultural, political, and economic trends, and concerns in the area of education reform during different periods. Daniel Sifuna and James Otiende note that after independence the main concerns of the Kenyan education system were how it could create national consciousness, adequate personnel to fill jobs left vacant by foreign expatriates, address societal needs, improve the quality of African education, and discover how it could be expanded and made accessible. In the early 1970s, it attempted to discover how to curb the increased levels of unemployment in the country and how to improve and enhance the quality of education. Between 1975 and 1985, the education system was more preoccupied with revising previous policies, creating new proposals about how to improve education, and working to ensure that the education offered was relevant to society's needs.[62] The late 1980s were marked with more revisions, curriculum reviews, and an enhancement of the quality of education. In the 1990s and 2000s, the main issues of concern have been how to improve quality, equity, and access to education. The chapter demonstrates the role of Gikubu in these educational transformations in both colonial and postcolonial Kenya through his work at SBC and the various roles he played there. He was a far-sighted leader who used various transformative educational and administrative approaches to foster youth education. To foreground his transformative educational approaches, Gikubu developed several educational and administrative strands that were instrumental to SBC's success both in academic subjects and in cocurricular areas. He sought to provide an education that was pragmatic, benefit based, attitude changing, holistic, service and virtue centered, democratic, and international.

NOTES

1. Kennedy Hongo and Jesse Mugambi, *Starehe Boys Centre: School and Institute. The First Forty Years 1959–1999* (Nairobi: Acton Publishers, 2003), 51.
2. Roger Martin, *Anthem of Bugles: The Story of Starehe Boys Centre and School* (Nairobi: Heinemann Educational Books Ltd., 1978).
3. Yusuf King'ala, *The Autobiography of Geoffrey William Griffin: Kenya's Champion Beggar* (Nairobi: Falcon Crest, 2005), 58.
4. King'ala, *The Autobiography of Geoffrey William Griffin: Kenya's Champion Beggar*, 59.
5. Ibid., 6.
6. Martin, *Anthem of Bugles: The Story of Starehe Boys Centre and School*, 19.
7. King'ala, *The Autobiography of Geoffrey William Griffin: Kenya's Champion Beggar*, 63.
8. Documentary Interview, Geoffrey Griffin, September 4, 2004.
9. King'ala, *The Autobiography of Geoffrey William Griffin: Kenya's Champion Beggar*, 64.
10. Ibid.
11. Documentary Interview, Geoffrey Griffin, September 4, 2004.
12. Interview, Joseph Gikubu, September 2, 2013.
13. Martin, *Anthem of Bugles: The Story of Starehe Boys Centre and School*, 4.
14. Interview, Joseph Gikubu, September 3, 2012.
15. Interview, Joseph Gikubu, September 4, 2012.
16. Interview, Joseph Gikubu, September 5, 2012.
17. Sorobea Bogonko, *A History of Modern Education in Kenya: 1895–1991* (Nairobi: Evans Brothers Limited), 69.
18. Bogonko, *A History of Modern Education in Kenya: 1895–1991*.
19. Daniel Sifuna and James Otiende, *An Introductory History of Education* (Nairobi: Nairobi University Press, 1992).
20. Daniel Sifuna and Ibrahim Oanda, *Historical and Contemporary Trends in the Development of Education in Kenya: Government Policy, Gender and Regional Dimensions* (Nairobi: The Jomo Kenyatta Foundation, 2014), 58.
21. Martin, *Anthem of Bugles: The Story of Starehe Boys Centre and School*, 11.
22. Interview, Joseph Gikubu, September 1, 2013.
23. Peter Ojiambo, *Teaching Beyond Teaching: Geoffrey William Griffin and Starehe Boys Centre and School* (Saarbrucken, Germany: VDM Verlag, 2008).
24. Documentary Interview, Geoffrey Griffin, September 4, 2004.

25. Martin, *Anthem of Bugles: The Story of Starehe Boys Centre and School*, 28.
26. Hongo and Mugambi, *Starehe Boys Centre: School and Institute. The First Forty Years 1959–1999*.
27. Ojiambo, *Teaching Beyond Teaching: Geoffrey William Griffin and Starehe Boys Centre and School*, 231.
28. Geoffrey Griffin's address to the Kenyan Council of Social Services in 1961 lamenting their inability to address the problem of youth vagrancy. The address gave a diagnosis of Starehe's challenges and the colonial educational realities of the time.
29. Hongo and Mugambi, *Starehe Boys Centre: School and Institute. The First Forty Years 1959–1999*, 97.
30. Television Interview, Geoffrey Griffin, May 6, 2000.
31. Interview, Joseph Gikubu, August 15, 2013.
32. Documentary Interview, Geoffrey Griffin, September 4, 2004.
33. Interview, Joseph Gikubu, July 18, 2012.
34. Martin, *Anthem of Bugles: The Story of Starehe Boys Centre and School*, 49.
35. Interview, Joseph Gikubu, August 19, 2013.
36. Television Interview, Geoffrey Griffin, May 6, 2000.
37. Ojiambo, *Teaching Beyond Teaching: Geoffrey William Griffin and Starehe Boys Centre and School*, 231.
38. Ibid.
39. Interview, Elizabeth Pamba, July 4, 2013.
40. Documentary Interview, Geoffrey Griffin, September 4, 2004.
41. Interview, Joseph Gikubu, July 8, 2012.
42. Television Interview, Geoffrey Griffin, May 6, 2000.
43. Ibid.
44. *Endeavor Magazine*, 1995, 3.
45. Ojiambo, *Teaching Beyond Teaching: Geoffrey William Griffin and Starehe Boys Centre and School*.
46. Documentary Interview, Geoffrey Griffin, September 4, 2004.
47. Interview, Edith Karaimu, September 3, 2013.
48. *Endeavor Magazine*, 1995, 17.
49. Interview, Peter Okono, June 29, 2005.
50. Sifuna and Otiende, *An Introductory History of Education*, 1992.
51. Ibid.
52. Ibid., 3.
53. Bogonko, *A History of Modern Education in Kenya: 1895–1991*.
54. Martin, *Anthem of Bugles: The Story of Starehe Boys Centre and School*, 112.
55. Ibid., 113.
56. King'ala, *The Autobiography of Geoffrey William Griffin: Kenya's Champion Beggar*, 173.
57. Ibid., 174.

58. Geoffrey Griffin's letter to Gikubu appreciating his role in physical training and the fame it had brought to SBC dated October 8, 1974.
59. Interview, Joseph Gikubu, August 25, 2012.
60. Interview, Joseph Gikubu, September 7, 2013.
61. Interview, Joseph Gikubu, September 8, 2013.
62. Daniel Sifuna and Ibrahim Oanda, *Historical and Contemporary Trends in the Development of Education in Kenya: Government Policy, Gender and Regional Dimensions.*

CHAPTER 6

Conclusion: Thoughts on Youth Education and School Leadership

Gikubu's views on Kenyan youth education and school leadership evolved over time, and many of them emanated from his experiences in Manyani, Wamumu, Othaya Approved School, and Starehe Boys Centre and School (SBC). Although originally not educated beyond junior high school, he spent most of his life in the sphere of education confronting many challenges that were experienced in Kenya in both the colonial and the postcolonial periods. From the onset of his involvement in Kenyan youth education, Gikubu realized that education was a central factor if the students they had taken under their care, drawn from deprived conditions, were to overcome their life challenges. It was not enough to offer them shelter, food, and medical care without equipping them with a high-quality education. From the start, their aim was to enable their students to build a ladder that would allow them move up to whatever level their intellectual capacities could propel them. Recalling their underlying purpose for engaging in education, Gikubu noted:

> Our first objective was to provide disadvantaged students with food, clothing, medical care and security. Once this was achieved, we had to think of their future. It was clear to us that only a first-rate education could ensure their long-term welfare. Therefore, we began to build an educational institution that could provide them with quality education.[1]

Gikubu and his other colleagues did not have any educational philosophy when they became involved in Kenyan youth education, but they knew they wanted to give their students the best education possible. To achieve this goal, they were ready to learn from all the key stakeholders, educational experts, their students, faculty, support staff, friends, administrators, and other schools within and outside Kenya. Describing their approach to creating a sound education system at SBC, Gikubu observed:

> My thoughts on education have developed over time from my long time engagement in education. When we began the school, I was more concerned with bringing students and giving them a sense of a normal disciplined life. During this time our main purpose was to provide them with essential survival skills. I knew however, that all our programs had to be quality if the students we had taken into our care were to do well in life.[2]

THOUGHTS ON YOUTH EDUCATION

Rich and Creative Education

Gikubu believed that an effective education system should be rich, creative, and critical. It was an education that was expected to provide students with a variety of approaches that would enable them to address the various challenges they would encounter in life. Commenting on Gikubu's constant urging that SBC students should be creative in handling various tasks in school, Beneah Kombe, an old student of SBC, said:

> Gikubu constantly reminded us *"tumia akili"* (use your brains) in addressing our various challenges at school. A good example that suffices here, is there was a time we ran out of brooms and we went to tell him that we could not do the cleaning that particular day because we lacked brooms. He quickly told us to be creative and to make brooms from sticks or use nice branches to sweep the paths as he planned to buy new ones later in the week. We took his advice and it worked. He was a strong believer in using creativity in addressing life challenges. Many of us have carried this philosophy to our careers.[3]

This approach to education enabled SBC to save a lot of money and also to devise various ways of improving its administrative and learning areas. Creativity with regard to making proper use of its meager resources has always been key in all SBC's operations. It has enabled the school to grow in both academic and cocurricular areas in the last five decades.

Incorporating African Indigenous Education in Contemporary Education

From the foundation of SBC, Gikubu wanted the school to incorporate central tenets of African indigenous education in its leadership work. Key among these were discipline, respect, a learning community, hard work, and reverence for the environment. Gikubu constantly urged Griffin and Geturo to ensure that SBC students were well grounded in African indigenous education. Commenting on the vitality of this in relation to SBC's educational mission, Gikubu observed:

> I wanted our students to imbibe, recognize and practice African values that I felt had guided me in my early years and had ensured there was harmony in society. I felt there was so much they could learn from that education that was essential in enabling them be successful people in life. Remember, African indigenous education trained us for life. I wanted the same reflected in the education that we were offering to our students. I am glad that we managed to achieve this.[4]

It was this incorporation of African indigenous education tenets, especially the discipline and holistic components, that led to SBC being recognized throughout Kenya in its early years. And it was by anchoring its educational work in these tenets that SBC was successful in both its academic and cocurricular activities.

Development-Centered Education

Gikubu and his colleagues believed that there were numerous youths in Kenya who were talented both in academic and in cocurricular areas and that there was need to tap into their various gifts in order to develop the country. For this belief to be realized students had to be offered a variety of academic and cocurricular subjects. Accordingly, Gikubu noted: "we wanted our students to acquire various skills that would enable them change their immediate communities and their country. It had to be a transformative and development-centered education."[5]

It was because of this that Gikubu insisted to his colleagues that various trades should be offered alongside regular education. Later he was instrumental in SBC's technical, accountancy, and computer education programs. He felt these were central to Kenya's national developmental process.

Holistic Education

Gikubu was a strong advocate of holistic education. He always urged his students to aim for excellence both inside and outside class. It was because of his firm support for holistic education that he was placed in charge of physical education. Commenting on the importance of holistic education, Gikubu said, "I did not want to produce students who were only good at academics and nothing else. I wanted to produce students who were masters of everything. I wanted my students to utilize their gifts in all areas of learning. I wanted them to enjoy their educational experience."[6]

Describing Gikubu's firm belief in holistic education, Elizabeth Pamba, a long-serving teacher at SBC, noted: "he had a dislike for students who were not active in sports or club activities. He insisted that each student must belong at least to one club and must be active in it. He argued that the nature of life is that we have to be holistic in all that we do."[7] This approach enabled SBC to invest equally in both academic subjects and cocurricular activities and to excel in both.

Nationalistic Education

For Gikubu education was expected to foster a spirit of nationalism among students. He wanted his students to develop love for their country and their fellow citizens. Recalling Gikubu's advice to them to be patriotic, Paul Jisas, an old student of SBC, remarked:

> He wanted us to be ready to serve our country in various ways including defending and even dying for it. He always gave his own example and his participation in Kenya's independence struggle when he was a teenager and much younger than most of us. He challenged us to have zeal for improving our country and serving it in various capacities.[8]

Explaining further his rationale for his students to acquire education that was nationalistic, Gikubu noted:

It was going to be impossible for my students to be responsible citizens and make meaningful changes in society if they did not love their societies and the nation. This required them to acquire skills that would enable them develop a nationalistic outlook, engagement and personal sacrifice to their country. Devotion and patriotism has to be a vital component of any sound and effective education.[9]

He wanted his students to be patriotic in their careers and to strive to make a difference. He argued that this was the only way they would help needy people in society or aspire to make a difference in society. He expected his students to have nationalistic ideals that went beyond individual gains. It was in this regard that he was a strong advocate of SBC's national voluntary community service that takes place yearly during students' vacation period.

Prudence and Efficient Management of School Resources

Gikubu believed in the proper and careful utilization of school resources. He was always searching for ways in which the school could cut its expenditure in all its financial planning. Having served as the deputy director, in charge of boarding for over five decades, he had developed financial skills and networks that enabled SBC to save funds in its boarding operations. Commenting on Gikubu's prudence, Martin Kamba, one of the longest serving administrators, observed:

> Without Gikubu it would have been difficult for us to manage in those early difficult years when we had limited donor funding and local resources. He was so efficient in ensuring that our meagre resources were well utilized. He was the force behind our financial stability. He knew how to cut unnecessary expenditures.[10]

Frank Ngugi, an alumnus of SBC and a former teacher at the school, recalled Gikubu's stringent financial measures:

> One day we were planning a one-day trip. I took the budget to him on the items we wanted for the trip. He went through the list item by item deleting several of them saying we were boys and we didn't need much. Bread, soda and water was enough for the day. He kept reminding us that our school is for the poor and we cannot afford any luxuries. He was meticulous on various ways of saving money.[11]

When it came to financial prudence Gikubu was clear, tough, and efficient. He insisted that as SBC was a school for the poor, it was essential that prudence should be applied in all its financial planning and expenditures. He argued that it was important for the school to live within its means and to plan wisely for its future using its meager resources.

Entrepreneurial Education

Gikubu advocated for an education that would make SBC students entrepreneurial. He believed that beyond just earning a salary, it was vital that people invested their money wisely and prudently. Using his personal example, he argued:

> Yes, I earn a salary. Yes, I work for Starehe but I have a family and a life outside Starehe that must be well planned and invested for. I want my students to learn skills that can make them survive beyond earning a salary. We live in tough financial times and we must prepare students to live in them. They cannot afford to live from hand to mouth. It is important that we incorporate entrepreneurial skills in our education system. They are essential both for individual and societal growth.[12]

He underscored that it was important for students to get an education that could make them entrepreneurial in various ways, noting that we live in times where these skills are not taught at all in many schools and yet are essential in life. Gikubu believed that students should be trained for the outside world. It was this view of education that saw him urge SBC to start courses in entrepreneurial fields, such as commerce, accountancy, and computer studies, and also to form a company that could market SBC's products.

Passion and Commitment to Youth Education

Gikubu emphasized the importance of youth education. According to him, a good education had to instill passion and commitment into young people so that they excelled in various areas of life. An effective education would enable youths to use their talents to serve society. He argued that the process was not easy as it required sacrifice, a long-time commitment to the process, and adequate resources. Using his own personal example, he urged his students to get interested in youth education early in life and to render service to those who were in difficult circumstances. He argued that "the youths are keepers and saviors of our communities. They deserve a sound education. We have no choice but to provide them with skills that can enable them realize this."[13] It was this commitment to youth education that saw him donate part of his salary to SBC for many years, to help educate poorer students—as illustrated in this communication from him to Griffin indicating his inability to continue with the donation owing to a tragedy that had occurred in his family. He wrote:

> As you know for many years, I have donated part of my monthly salary to the school to enable needy students' access education. I have done this until December, 2004. You are also aware that my daughter passed away on December 10th, 2004 leaving a 5-year-old girl child. I am now fully responsible for her education, up-bringing and upkeep. In the said circumstances, I find myself overburdened and it is no longer easy for me to continue with the monthly donations.[14]

He noted that it was vital to provide youths with a rich and high-quality education; an education that would sensitize them to critical societal needs and enable them to aspire to transform society.

THOUGHTS ON SCHOOL LEADERSHIP

Gikubu spent 55 years as a senior administrator at SBC and worked assiduously until his death in 2014, aged 80. Commenting on his long involvement, he noted: "I love working with the youth. Their success always excites me. I have been around youths for so long that I cannot imagine my life without them."[15] Owing to his long engagement in youth education and school leadership in general, he developed insightful administrative principles that I will discuss here in some detail.

Purpose-Driven Leadership

For school leadership to be effective, according to Gikubu, a school is expected to stipulate its goals and objectives at its inception and work consistently to ensure that that its purpose and vision are understood and maintained by all relevant stakeholders. For him it was clear from the foundation of SBC that its mandate was to offer a transformative education to disadvantaged youths. It was from this source that all its educational and administrative approaches and ethos sprang. Regarding its purpose-driven leadership, Gikubu noted: "we wanted to change lives of the needy youths and our school leadership approaches had to reflect this. We expected all the other pertinent stakeholders that worked with us to articulate and practice this."[16] He advised students to keep the school motto "Natulenge Juu" (Aim High) in their work once they discovered their true purpose or career in life.

Gikubu wanted his students to acquire an education that would enable them to discover their purpose in life and enable them to strive towards it. This required SBC to work closely with its students to nurture their various gifts and nudge them to use those gifts to develop society.

Longevity in School Leadership

Effective school leadership requires the headteacher and other school leaders' long engagement with school administration. Expressing Gikubu's views on the subject, Elizabeth Pamba noted:

> Gikubu believed that administrators and teachers should work long enough and if not a lifetime in their schools. To him, this was essential for it provided the school sound institutional memory that was crucial in creating excellence in all areas of learning. Further, long engagement with school leadership according to Gikubu created confidence, understanding and deep love for the school since it is impossible to stay in one place for so many years if you don't like it.[17]

This belief was evident in all SBC's school leaders, teachers, and support staff. Many of them stayed at SBC their entire working life. Several of them had stayed at SBC for over 30 years and were very proud of the institution. Staff longevity was the cornerstone to much of SBC's success and growth.

Open Management System

Gikubu believed that an effective school leadership system should be open in nature and should be void of unnecessary bureaucracy. He advocated for free access of students, faculty, and staff to his office. This administrative principle made the handling of day-to-day activities easier and faster. He argued: "an open door policy makes school operations faster, spontaneous, transparent and more interactive. It has been the cornerstone of our success."[18] This administrative approach made SBC into a more close-knit family and very effective in its delivery of services to students, faculty, staff, parents, donors, and visitors.

This administrative style was evident in all aspects of SBC's work, and it was rare for matters to be delayed or for appointments to see Gikubu or other members of senior management to be denied.

Creating a Strong Bond with the Alumni

Gikubu believed in the power of SBC's alumni to change the school. For him, SBC belonged to its alumni and it was through them that its work and ethos was to live on. Because of this, he maintained close ties with SBC alumni and was a regular presence at many of their functions, especially Starehe Old Boys Society annual gatherings. On many occasions, they visited him at school or invited him to personal events such as weddings or birthdays. Commenting on Gikubu's love for the SBC alumni, Peter Nganga, an alumnus of the school, remarked:

> Gikubu loved us and we loved him. He constantly reminded us to ensure that we don't forget the benefits we have received from the school. It was our duty to ensure that we help others to enjoy the same privileges. He was devoted to the success of the school. His devotion to the school challenged us to do the same. He wanted our bond as old students to be kept. To him we were one big loving family.[19]

He constantly challenged SBC alumni to ensure they carry on the legacy of SBC and to see to it that they committed their time or finances to SBC's mission, as others had done to educate them. Echoing Gikubu's words and urging its alumni to carry this torch forward, Josphat Mwaura, the current chairperson of the Old Starehian Society and a member of its Managing Committee, noted:

> Today Starehe needs its alumni more than ever before. None of the current students have experienced all the three founder directors. It is up to the alumni to share the experiences of these founders with the later generations of alumni and students and in that way, sustain the Starehe Way. Above all, Starehe needs the Old Boys who have been transformed from poverty to prosperity to give back to their alma mater. Every Old Boy needs to demonstrate at least three things: that they are paid up and are active members of OSS; that they are actively contributing to Starehe either financially or in time commitments; and that wherever they are, they are maintaining the good

name of Starehe by providing exemplary leadership and transforming the society we live in. The Starehe founders taught us that even the most difficult human beings have some goodness in them, they have aspirations for their lives, they can perform if equipped, and above all, they can make a positive contribution to the world."[20]

Individual Attention, Love, and Care for Students

Gikubu believed in an individual-centered, loving, and caring administration. As the person in charge of SBC's boarding section, he spent much of his time attending to students and staff matters and was keen, caring, loving, and patient. He granted each student and staff individual attention. Roger Martin writes: "he paid much attention to each individual. In fact it was his attention to detail, both human and administrative, care, and love which enabled him to shape his students' attitude to life and enabled Starehe to excel in every area."[21]

Further, Gikubu also advocated for a leadership that nurtures love and care among students. He argued that a school that creates a loving and caring community creates opportunities for all to excel. He noted: "a school that creates habits of love and care among its faculty, students, and the larger community cannot fail in its learning and teaching mission. This has been our mantra at Starehe and the basis of much of our success. We love and provide great care to our students and they have responded likewise to work."[22]

Partnering in School Leadership

Gikubu believed that an effective school leadership entailed creating strong partnerships with all the relevant stakeholders, namely: faculty, administrators, support staff, students, and donors. He believed in collective leadership and valued the input of every stakeholder in addressing SBC's challenges. He argued: "a successful school must tap into the talents of its stakeholders. You need the help of so many people to do well. This has been our strength over the years. We have benefited from the help of so many people over the years."[23] Much of SBC's growth and success has emanated from its strong partnering approach to leadership.

Gikubu was keen to ensure that these partnerships were maintained in SBC and he constantly ensured that there was regular communication and meetings with all SBC partners. Further, he was constantly searching for new partners.

Relationality in School Leadership

Gikubu believed that a good school should strive to establish firm human relations both within and outside the school. He viewed this as a vehicle for a school's success. It is because of this that he ensured SBC maintained strong relationships with a number of its present and former administrators, teachers, and donors. These played a vital role in enabling several of SBC's staff to stay on for many years and helped to give the school financial security and growth.

SBC has built other relationships with its students. Gikubu ensured that SBC students stayed close to the school and established enduring ties. He also ensured that SBC maintained mutual links with its former students, both at individual and group level, through the Old Boys Society. Beyond the school community, Gikubu also forged close relations with SBC's financial donors at governmental, individual, and corporate levels. He ensured that those who had assisted the school for many years were immortalized in the school in some way, either by having a building named after them or by having their portraits displayed in key areas.

Servant Leadership

Gikubu viewed school leadership as servant leadership. To him leadership was a calling that required passion, conviction, vision, devotion, humility, competence, clarity of thought, action, personal sacrifice, sincerity, integrity, patriotism, and collaboration. He emphasized that a school head was expected to lead by example. Although the head could delegate some duties, he/she was required to be central to the school leadership and to be knowledgeable about all its workings, happenings, and planning.

Using his own example, he argued that servant leadership entailed a lot of sacrifice, hard work, and minimal financial rewards. He remarked: "a good school leader has to view his work as a noble profession, a higher calling that money cannot pay. School leaders who view their work in this regard succeed in all areas for they work over and above their appointment mandates and time limits."[24] It was this conceptualization of leadership that made Gikubu to work at SBC beyond his retirement age. His was a response to a higher calling, vision, and mission. His singular determination, diligence, and dedication to the work of Kenyan youth education was clear and admirable.

Commitment to Community Engagement

Gikubu was a strong advocate of community engagement. He encouraged SBC to be involved in community service right from its founding. Each year he looked for more ways in which SBC students could help the community. It was because of his firm belief in community engagement that he established the Starehe Voluntary Service Scheme, where each holiday SBC students would provide free voluntary service throughout Kenya. Throughout his five decades of working at SBC, the school was involved in much community engagement, for instance raising money for victims of hunger, flood, or fire.

Calling for stronger links between school and communities, Gikubu noted: "schools exist in communities and it is not possible for them to divorce their educational work from their communities. After all, where will students work when they finish their studies? An effective educational undertaking must endeavor to link its work to community needs."[25] It was this leadership approach that brought SBC's educational mission to public attention both inside and outside Kenya.

Conclusion

This book demonstrates that Gikubu's involvement in Kenyan youth education was not influenced by one single force, but rather it was influenced by the prevailing historical conditions that placed many Kenyan youths in societal limbo during the colonial period. Gikubu's direct engagement in youth education can be traced to Manyani, Wamumu, and Othaya, although it grew to full standing at SBC. Whatever else Gikubu accomplished in the field, his greatest legacy is embodied in SBC. It is here, owing to his indefatigable efforts, that more than 60,000 youths have been able to receive quality education. Their contribution to national development in the last six decades has been enormous. It is clear from the foregoing that Gikubu was an exceptional school leader and a tireless champion of Kenyan youth education. His educational initiatives, administrative approaches, and sacrifices were all aimed at empowering and liberating disadvantaged youths from illiteracy and poverty. However, he was not a "lone ranger." His involvement in Kenyan youth education was only possible because of the support he received from various colleagues, especially Griffin and Geturo, as well as donor agencies and the Kenyan government.

A critical examination of Gikubu's contributions to Kenyan youth education demonstrates the power of the human spirit in effecting societal change and the role of biographies in illuminating critical societal issues. It demonstrates, according to Chinua Achebe, "the potency of the unpredictable in human affairs and the power of the human spirit to resist an abridgement of its humanity."[26] Gikubu was such a spirit: a strong spirit who rose from the ashes of Manyani and Wamumu detention camps to the pinnacle of Kenyan youth education. It was this spirit and his 55-year contribution that make his portrait a great Kenyan and African education story. Affirming this, Josphat Mwaura writes:

> Gikubu's story is especially inspirational. It is a story of a life that is worthy of study by every young man in Kenya. It is a life that demonstrates the success that can be achieved irrespective of the hand you get dealt in life. It is a story of a teenager filled with passion for his country, invested with the purpose of transforming the youth, consumed by the need to actively engage in whatever task he is called to perform. Above all, it is a story of faith in the human race. From Banana to Manyani to Wamumu to Starehe and finally to his resting place in Juja, Gikubu's life demonstrated that there is nothing anyone can do to you to break your resolve or human dignity. You can bring change for the better, wherever you are, no matter your skills or circumstances. Success in life depends on your faith and beliefs, on your revealed purpose, on your passion, on your hard work, and on your persistence until excellence and the promise are delivered.[27]

I would like to conclude this book with the words of Roger Martin, Assistant Director of SBC (1969–1979). Martin wrote: "Gikubu's work is great educational work that transformative educational leaders can learn from. Time is not on our side. An achievement like this deserves our attention, research, and documentation."[28] This book demonstrates the extent to which Gikubu's contributions to Kenyan youth education deserve to be known and understood. Very few educators with his level of education have given so much to the education field as he did—not just in Africa but anywhere in the world.

Notes

1. Interview, Joseph Gikubu, August 11, 2012.
2. Interview, Joseph Gikubu, August 11, 2013.
3. Interview, Beneah Kombe, August 3, 2012.

4. Interview, Joseph Gikubu, August 16, 2013.
5. Interview, Joseph Gikubu, August 12, 2013.
6. Interview, Joseph Gikubu, July 30, 2012.
7. Interview, Elizabeth Pamba, July 7, 2013.
8. Interview, Paul Jisas, July 2, 2012.
9. Interview, Joseph Gikubu, August 25, 2013.
10. Interview, Martin Kamba, July 15, 2013.
11. Interview, Frank Ngugi, August 19, 2013.
12. Interview, Joseph Gikubu, August 26, 2013.
13. Interview, Joseph Gikubu, July 28, 2013.
14. A letter from Joseph Gikubu to Geoffrey Griffin dated January 6, 2005 indicating his inability to continue funding needy students at Starehe Boys Centre and School owing to a tragedy that had occurred in his family.
15. Interview, Joseph Gikubu, July 9, 2013.
16. Interview, Joseph Gikubu, August 22, 2012.
17. Interview, Elizabeth Pamba, July 29, 2013.
18. Interview, Joseph Gikubu, July 28, 2012.
19. Interview, Peter Nganga, July 21, 2012.
20. An article in the *Daily Nation* newspaper from Josphat Mwaura, the then chairperson of Old Starehian Society and a member of its Managing Committee, dated July 13, 2015, urging old boys of the school to get involved in its activities and to help the disadvantaged in society.
21. Roger Martin, *Anthem of Bugles: The Story of Starehe Boys Centre and School* (Nairobi: Heinemann Educational Books Ltd., 1978), 31.
22. Interview, Joseph Gikubu, July 11, 2012.
23. Interview, Joseph Gikubu, July 29, 2012.
24. Interview, Joseph Gikubu, August 9, 2013.
25. Interview, Joseph Gikubu, August 3, 2012.
26. Chinua Achebe, *The Education of a British-protected Child* (New York: Alfred A. Knopf, 2009), 23.
27. An article in the *Daily Nation* newspaper from Josphat Mwaura, July 13, 2015.
28. Martin, *Anthem of Bugles: The Story of Starehe Boys Centre and School*, viii.

References

Abagi, Okwach, and Ibrahim Ogachi. 2014. *Fifty Years of Education Development in Kenya: Mapping Out the Gains, Challenges and Prospects for the Future*. Nairobi: The Jomo Kenyatta Foundation.

Achebe, Chinua. 2009. *The Education of a British-Protected Child*. New York: Alfred A. Knopf.

Adeoti, Ezekiel. 1997. *Alayande as Educationist 1948–1983: A Study of Alayande's Contribution to Education and Social Change*. Ibadan: Educational Books.

Ajayi, Jacob. 1990. *History and the Nation and Other Addresses*. Ibadan: Spectrum Books.

Berman, Bruce. 1990. *Control and Crisis in Colonial Kenya: The Dialectic of Domination*. London: James Currey.

Bogonko, Sorobea. 1992. *A History of Modern Education in Kenya, 1895–1992*. Nairobi: Evans Brothers.

Carr, Edward. 1961. *What is History?* London: Pelican.

Coker, Francis. 1973. *The Rt. Revd. Seth Irunsewe Kale*. Lagos: C.S.S. Press.

Colony and Protectorate of Kenya. 1953. *Ministry of Community Development Annual Reports, WAMYOU/G/14/35*. Nairobi: Kenya National Archives.

———. 1954a. *African Affairs Department Annual Reports, 33/333/11/77A*. Nairobi: Kenya National Archives.

———. 1954b. *Ministry of Community Development Annual Reports, MCD/ADM/61/60*. Nairobi: Kenya National Archives.

———. 1955a. *Ministry of Community Development Annual Reports, WAMYOU/G/6/2*. Nairobi: Kenya National Archives.

———. 1955b. *Ministry of Community Development Annual Reports, WAMYOU/G/6/28*. Nairobi: Kenya National Archives.

———. 1955c. *Ministry of Community Development Annual Reports, WAMYOU/ G/20/13*. Nairobi: Kenya National Archives.

———. 1956a. *Ministry of Community Development Annual Reports, APPR/PUB/ 1/1/1/25*. Nairobi: Kenya National Archives.

———. 1956b. *Ministry of Community Development Annual Reports, CD/36/14/ 56*. Nairobi: Kenya National Archives.

———. 1956c. *Ministry of Community Development Annual Reports, CRD/ADM/ 61/60*. Nairobi: Kenya National Archives.

———. 1956d. *Ministry of Community Development Annual Reports, WAMYOU/ G/21/92*. Nairobi: Kenya National Archives.

———. 1957a. *Prisons Department, Annual Reports, ADM/61/47*. Nairobi: Kenya National Archives.

———. 1957b. *African Affairs Department Annual Reports, 43/10A/57*. Nairobi: Kenya National Archives.

———. 1957c. *African Affairs Department Annual Reports, 145/1957*. Nairobi: Kenya National Archives.

———. 1957d. *Ministry of Community Development Annual Reports, CD/NY/3/ 1/1957*. Nairobi: Kenya National Archives.

———. 1957e. *Ministry of Community Development Annual Reports, CYC/POL/ 8/1957*. Nairobi: Kenya National Archives.

———. 1957f. *Ministry of Community Development Annual Reports, CYO/POL/5/ 1957*. Nairobi: Kenya National Archives.

———. 1957g. *Ministry of Community Development Annual Reports, EMER.45/ 13/1/14A-196*. Nairobi: Kenya National Archives.

———. 1957h. *Ministry of Community Development Annual Reports, POL/40/3/ 1957*. Nairobi: Kenya National Archives.

———. 1957i. *Ministry of Community Development Annual Reports, PRIS/25/6/1/ 70*. Nairobi: Kenya National Archives.

———. 1958a. *Ministry of Community Development Annual Reports, CYC/COL/ GEN/30/1958*. Nairobi: Kenya National Archives.

———. 1958b. *Ministry of Community Development Annual Reports, CYC/CP/ GEN/53*. Nairobi: Kenya National Archives.

———. 1958c. *Ministry of Community Development Annual Reports, CYC/CP/ GEN/FH/16*. Nairobi: Kenya National Archives.

———. 1958d. *Ministry of Community Development Annual Reports, CYC/KAYC/ORG/49*. Nairobi: Kenya National Archives.

———. 1958e. *Ministry of Community Development Annual Reports, CYO/MR/3/ 1958*. Nairobi: Kenya National Archives.

———. 1958f. *Ministry of Community Development Annual Reports, NY/3/1/ 1958*. Nairobi: Kenya National Archives.

———. 1958g. *Ministry of Community Development Annual Reports, WAMYOU/ G/29/329*. Nairobi: Kenya National Archives.

———. 1958h. *Ministry of Community Development Annual Reports, WAMYOU/ SEC/POL/32.* Nairobi: Kenya National Archives.

———. 1958i. *Ministry of Community Development Annual Reports, Y/40/2/1/58.* Nairobi: Kenya National Archives.

———. 1960. *Ministry of Community Development Annual Reports, MCD/10/1/8/ 1960.* Nairobi: Kenya National Archives.

Creswell, John. 1998. *Qualitative Inquiry and Research Design.* Thousand Oaks: Sage.

Denzin, Norman, and Lincoln Yvonna. 2000. *Handbook of Qualitative Research.* Thousand Oaks: Sage.

District Commissioners Reports. 1959. *DC/EMB/2/1/1.* Embu: Embu District.

———. 1960. *DC/GRSSA/7/22.* Garissa: Garissa District.

Elkins, Caroline. 2005. *Imperial Reckoning: The Untold Story of Britain's Gulag in Kenya.* New York: Henry Holt and Company.

Eshiwani, George. 1993. *Education in Kenya Since Independence.* Nairobi: East African Publishers.

Griffin, Geoffrey. 1958. *Ministry of Community Development Reports, VQ/21/2.* Nairobi: Kenya National Archives.

———. 1996. *School Mastery: Straight Talk About Boarding School Management.* Nairobi: Lectern Publications.

Hickley, Henry. 1957. *Ministry of Health Report, 43/10B/57.* Nairobi: Kenya National Archives.

Hongo, Kennedy, and Mugambi Jesse. 2003. *Starehe Boys Centre: School and Institute. The First Forty Years 1959–1999.* Nairobi: Acton Publishers.

Kanogo, Tabitha. 1987. *Squatters and the Roots of Mau Mau.* London: James Currey.

King'ala, Yusuf. 2005. *The Autobiography of Geoffrey William Griffin: Kenya's Champion Beggar.* Nairobi: Falcon Crest.

Kipkorir, Benjamin. 1980. *Biographical Essays on Imperialism and Colonialism in Colonial Kenya.* Nairobi: Kenya Literature Bureau.

Kridel, Craig. 1988. *Writing Educational Biography: Explorations in Qualitative Research.* New York: Garland.

Martin, Roger. 1978. *Anthem of Bugles: The Story of Starehe Boys Centre and School.* Nairobi: Heinemann Educational.

Mba, Edward. 1990. *Ayo Rosiji: Man with Vision.* Ibadan: Spectrum Books.

Ministry of Community Development. 1957. *Annual Reports, AB/16/19.* Nairobi: Kenya National Archives.

———. 1958. *Annual Report, AB/4/44.* Nairobi: Kenya National Archives.

Ministry of Health. 1955. *Annual Reports, AB/2/62.* Nairobi: Kenya National Archives.

Ministry of Labour. 1961. *Report of a Survey of Problems of Child Welfare in Kenya, BZ/5/9.* Nairobi: Kenya National Archives.

Ocobock, Paul. 2006. Joy Rides for Juveniles: Vagrant Youth and Colonial Control in Nairobi, Kenya, 1901–1952. *Social History* 31 (1): 39–59.
Odhiambo, Atieno, and Lonsdale John. 2003. *Mau Mau and Nationhood: Arms, Authority and Narration*. Athens: Ohio University Press.
Ojiambo, Peter. 2008. *Teaching Beyond Teaching: Geoffrey William Griffin and Starehe Boys Centre and School*. Saarbrucken: VDM Verlag.
Personnel Office. 1960. *Annual Reports, OP/1/1017*. Nairobi: Kenya National Archives.
Republic of Kenya. 1949. *Beecher Report on African Education in Kenya*. Nairobi: Government Printer.
———. 1958a. *Kenya Association of Youth Clubs Manual*. Nairobi: Government Printer.
———. 1958b. *The Constitution of Kenya Association of Youth Clubs*. Nairobi: Government Printer.
Sifuna, Daniel, and Otiende James. 1992. *An Introductory History of Education*. Nairobi: Nairobi University Press.
Sifuna, Daniel, and Ibrahim Oanda. 2014. *Historical and Contemporary Trends in the Development of Education in Kenya: Government Policy, Gender and Regional Dimensions*. Nairobi: The Jomo Kenyatta Foundation.
Smith, Arnold. 1966. *Social Change: Social Theory and Historical Processes*. London: Longman.
Starehe Boys Centre and School. 1995. *Endeavor Magazine*. Nairobi: Government Printer.
Thiong'o, Ngugi Wa. 1993. *Moving the Centre: The Struggles for Cultural Freedoms*. Oxford: James Currey.
United Nations. 1948. *Rights of Children*. New York: United Nations.
Weekly Digest Magazine. 1957. *Sunday Magazine*. Nairobi: Nation Newspapers.

Index

A
academic and cocurricular, 171
accountancy, 152
administrative, 151
African biographies, 3
African citizenry, 63
African district councils, 74
African family, 81
African indigenous education, 171
African youth, 120
agriculture, 53
alumni, 177
approved schools, 14, 45
artisan courses, 158
askaris, 39
Askwith, Thomas, 25

B
Baraza, 8, 53
Baring, Evelyn, Governor, 120
Beecher Report, 81
biographies, 1

C
care, 178
character, 133

character training, 59
child vagrancy, 105
citizenship, 36, 81
civics, 81
club committees, 103
collaborators, 60
colonial, 2
colonial citizens, 59
colonial government, 35
colonial state, 81
colony, 66
colony youth organizer, 74
commitment, 174
Community Development, 143
community development officer, 97
community engagement, 180
community service, 98
computer studies, 152
cottage industries, 86
counterinsurgency, 24
counterrevolution, 30
creative, 170

D
delinquents, 74
delinquent youths, 88
detainees, 60

detention, 9
development-centered education, 171
Diment, Don, 82
discipline, 171
district officer, 97
donor funding, 159
Dulverton Trust, 103

E
East Africa Certificate of Education, 154
education, 3
educational biography, 2
educational leadership, 4
Elkins, Caroline, 9
emergency villages, 65
Empire Youth Movement, 36, 80
entrepreneurial, 174
Eton of Africa, 62
Europeans, 129
expatriates, 143
experts, 142

F
Ford Foundation, 138
freedom, 54

G
Gardner, George, 47
Geturo, Geoffrey, 125
Gikubu, Joseph, 1, 125
government policy, 142
Grant in Aid, 94
Griffin, Geoffrey William, 36

H
handicrafts, 96
hardcore youths, 50
hearts and minds, 23

holistic, 171
holistic education, 172
Houwer, Mulock, 146
Hughes, Dorothy, 125, 143
human relations, 179

I
independence, 120
individual-centered, 178
infrastructure, 157
institutions, 142
International Labor Organization, 159

J
juvenile criminals, 67
juvenile delinquency, 32
Juvenile reception centers, 14, 122
juvenile vagrants, 71

K
Kamiti, 34
Kariokor Youth Club, 126
Kenya, 65
Kenya Association of Youth Clubs, 122
Kenya Junior of Secondary Education, 153
Kenya Junior Secondary Examinations, 153
Kenya Primary Examinations, 141
Kenya Prisons Department, 132
Kenyan secondary education, 132
Kikuyu reserves, 59
Kikuyu youths, 59

L
labor projects, 105
land, 59
land consolidation, 82

Langata, 34
large clubs, 102
Legislative Council, 125
literacy classes, 109
literacy courses, 98
locational councils, 103
longevity, 176
love, 178

M
Maendeleo Ya Wanawake, 85
Malaya, 24
Manyani Detention Camp, 23
Martin, Roger, 148
Mathira Division, 83–4
Mau Mau, 7
Mau Mau disease, 58
Mau Mau movement, 9
Mau Mau War, 9, 120
Mboya, Thomas, 125
Meru District, 87
Ministry of Education, 151
modern civilization, 83
modernity, 81
Moll, Peter, 82

N
Nairobi, 120
national development, 158
nationalism, 172
nationalist movement, 120
Njenga, Peter, 125
Nottingham, John, 89, 122

O
oathing, 87
occupation, 138

old boys' society, 53
Old Starehian Society, 177
Ominde Commission, 158
Operation Anvil, 12
Operation Jock Scott, 9
orphans, 67
Othaya Approved School, 73
Oxford Committee for Famine Relief, 139
Owles, Roger, 47, 73

P
partnering, 178
passion, 174
physical training, 162
pilot programs, 87
pipeline, 29
places of safety, 69
political propaganda, 63
postcolonial, 2
primary, 136
propaganda, 60
prudence, 173
purpose-driven leadership, 176
The Purpose of a Youth Club, 95–6

R
recreational programs, 86
re-education, 59
registration, 139
rehabilitation, 9
rehabilitation camp, 45
remand homes, 69
repatriation, 29, 69
rescue, 134
reserves, 101
reunions, 53
rich, 170

roundups, 71
Rural youth club, 86

S
Save the Children Fund, 144
school leadership, 169
scouting, 53
secondary, 136
self-supporting, 96
servant leadership, 179
Service and High Endeavor, 94
Shaw, Patrick, 148
Sheikh Trust, 104
Shell/BP, 124
skilled workforce, 152
Slade, Godfrey, 89
social hall, 97
Social Welfare, 141
societal development, 98
sorting houses, 70
spiritual activities, 53
Starehe Boys Centre and School (SBC), 1
Starehe Youth Club, 124
State of Emergency, 9
student freedom, 53
Swynerton Plan, 82

T
technical, 150
technical education, 152
technical schools, 154
tertiary education, 152
trade tests, 138
trades, 40
transformative, 171
transformative education, 175
transit camps, 70

transit home, 144
truants, 67
Truth and Loyalty, 62

U
unemployment, 88
urban migration, 86
urban vagrancy, 80

V
vagabondage, 79
vagrancy, 12
villagization, 13, 82
vocational, 153
voluntary community service, 173
voluntary leadership, 102
volunteers, 148
volunteer staff, 150

W
Waigwa, George, 125
Wamumu Rehabilitation Camp, 7, 45
welfare, 97
Western civilization, 81
Whitehouse, Paul, 149
Women's Progress, 85
work camps, 19, 45

Y
youth camps, 14, 45
youth club leaders, 91
youth clubs, 14, 79
youth education, 1, 120
Youth Help Campaigns, 125
youth vagrancy, 16

The manufacturer's authorised representative in the EU is Springer Nature Customer Service Centre GmbH, Europaplatz 3, 69115 Heidelberg, Germany. If you have any concerns regarding our products, please contact ProductSafety@springernature.com

Printed and bound by CPI Group (UK) Ltd, Croydon, CR0 4YY

23/03/2026

02076735-0002